SMALL CLAIMS H

AUSTRALIA
Law Book Co.
Sydney

CANADA and USA
Carswell
Toronto

HONG KONG
Sweet & Maxwell Asia

NEW ZEALAND
Brookers
Wellington

SINGAPORE and MALAYSIA
Sweet & Maxwell Asia
Singapore and Kuala Lumpur

SMALL CLAIMS HANDBOOK
(2nd EDITION)

W.C.H. Ervine, B.A., LL.B. (Dub.),
LL.M. (Lon.)

Senior Lecturer in Law at the
University of Dundee

THOMSON
™
W. GREEN

Published in 2003 by
W. Green & Son Ltd
21 Alva Street
Edinburgh EH2 4PS

www.wgreen.co.uk

Typeset by Interactive Sciences Ltd, Gloucester
Printed and bound in Great Britain by TJ International Ltd,
Padstow, Cornwall

No natural forests were destroyed to make this product;
only farmed timber was used and replanted

A CIP catalogue record for this book is available from
the British Library.

ISBN 0414 01206 2

For Carol and Jonathon

PREFACE TO SECOND EDITION

The second edition appears 13 years after the first not because it would not have been justified earlier by developments but because it seemed sensible to await the new rules which tantalisingly seemed to be in the offing. New rules are now in place although, surprisingly, changes in the financial limits have not been introduced at the same time. Scotland thus has the doubtful distinction of having the lowest ceiling for small claims in the UK. In Northern Ireland the limit is £2,000 and in England it is £5,000, except for personal injury cases where it is £1,000.

I am grateful to a number of people for their help. Several solicitors sent me transcripts of cases in which they had been involved. I have also had the benefit of discussions with sheriffs, solicitors, court staff and other officials, trading standards officers and advice agency staff who have had day to day involvement with small claims procedure. When it first seemed likely that a new edition would be produced, Ms Carly Neild, then an undergraduate in the Faculty of Law at Dundee University, gave valuable help. Neil McKinlay of Greens tactfully applied pressure to extract a manuscript and Rebecca Standing has expertly seen it through the publishing process.

I have attempted to state the law as at December 18, 2002, though it has proved possible to add some later material.

COWAN ERVINE

April 2003

PREFACE TO FIRST EDITION

Numerous sheriffs, solicitors, court staff and litigants who have been willing to discuss the small claims procedure with me have been helpful in preparing this book. My debt to Sheriff Macphail's *Sheriff Court Practice* is evident on many pages. I am especially grateful to my colleague Professor Bill McBryde, and to Roger Bland and Billy McCulloch of the Scottish Courts Administration who took the trouble to read Chapters 2 to 6. They made valuable suggestions for their improvement and saved me from a number of errors. I am also indebted to Peter Nicholson who encouraged me to write in the first place and provided me with transcripts of unreported judgments. I have attempted to state the law as at November 1, 1990, though it has been possible to incorporate some changes which took place after that date.

COWAN ERVINE

Hogmanay, 1990

CONTENTS

PART 1—GUIDE TO SMALL CLAIM PROCEDURE

PART 2—LEGISLATION

TABLE OF CASES

TABLE OF STATUTES

TABLE OF STATUTORY INSTRUMENTS

SMALL CLAIM RULES 2002

TABLE OF ABBREVIATIONS

All E.R.	All England Law Reports
E.C.R.	European Court Reports
G.W.D.	Green Weekly Digest
(H.L.)	House of Lords
R.	Rettie
S.C.	Session Cases
S.C.C.R.	Scottish Criminal Case Reports
S.C.L.R.	Scottish Civil Law Reports
S.L.T.	Scots Law Times
(Sh. Ct.)	Sheriff Court

PART 1—GUIDE TO SMALL CLAIM PROCEDURE

CHAPTER 1

INTRODUCTION

Small claim procedure is now governed by the Act of Sederunt (Small Claim Rules) 2002 which introduced revised rules with effect from June 10, 2002. Before analysing these rules it is worth describing how this stage has been reached.

On Saint Andrew's Day 1988 one of the more radical changes in Scottish court procedure came into effect with the introduction of the small claim procedure in the sheriff court. The procedure is a form of summary cause process[1] and is intended to deal with a wide range of claims for up to £750. This brought the Scottish legal system into line with the other two law districts in the United Kingdom which have had small claim procedures for some years, as have many jurisdictions in the United States and the Commonwealth.

It is ironic that Scotland should in recent years have lagged behind the rest of the United Kingdom in this respect. In the late eighteenth and early nineteenth centuries the small claims issue frequently gained the attention of Parliament. An Act of 1795 created a Justice of the Peace Court which remained in existence, at least in some parts of Scotland, until 1971.[2] Two or more justices could hear causes relating to recovery of debts or the making effective of any demand where the debt did not exceed five pounds.

In 1825 "An Act for the more easily Recovery of Small Debts in the Sheriff Courts in Scotland"[3] was passed permitting sheriffs to hear "all civil causes and complaints . . . wherein the debt shall not exceed Eight Pounds Sterling, exclusive of expenses and fees of extract, in a summary way . . . ." Only four years later the Small Debts (Scotland) Act 1829 recorded that while this Act had proved beneficial, experience had shown how it could be improved. The major change in the 1829 Act increased the financial limit to £100. In both the 1825 and 1829 Acts stress was laid on achieving a simple procedure: there was to be no written record of the proceedings; and professional legal representation

---

[1] Sheriff Courts (Scotland) Act 1971, s.35(2).
[2] Small Debts (Scotland) Act 1795 and see *The Sheriff Court*, Cmnd. 3248 (1967). Hereafter the "Grant Committee."
[3] Small Debt (Scotland) Act 1825.

1

was all but prohibited. The 1829 Act was soon repealed by the Small Debt (Scotland) Act 1837 which reduced the financial ceiling for summary procedure to £8 6s. 8d. but retained the virtual prohibition on legal representation. Section 14 provided that "No Procurators, Solicitors nor any Person practising the Law shall be allowed to appear or plead for any Party without leave of the Court upon special cause shown".

The next major legislation affecting the sheriff court, the Sheriff Courts (Scotland) Act 1907 raised the financial limit for sheriff court small debt actions to £20. At the same time the summary civil cause with an upper limit of £50 was introduced. In 1963 this limit was raised to £250 while the debt limit was raised to £50.[4] This procedure provided for abbreviated pleadings with the possibility of dispensing with the recording of evidence. The Grant Committee, however, noted that its procedure has tended to become more elaborate over the years.[5]

The Grant Committee, the most recent committee to have reviewed the workings of the sheriff court, included amongst their recommendations a new summary procedure. This recommendation was implemented in the Sheriff Courts (Scotland) Act 1971,[6] which created and governs the summary cause procedure. The intention of the Grant Committee was to provide a procedure that was both cheap and efficient. It retained features of earlier sheriff court procedures in that it did not normally involve written pleadings and the lengthy adjustment procedure that takes place in the ordinary cause.

There is no recording of evidence at the hearing. The original financial limit was £1,000 but this was increased on November 30, 1988 to £1,500, which is also the extent of the sheriff court's privative jurisdiction.[7] Summary cause actions are actions for payment of money; actions of multiplepoinding where the value of the fund in dispute does not exceed £1,500; actions *ad factum praestandum* and actions for the recovery of possession of both heritable and moveable property; and proceedings which according to the law and practice existing immediately before the commencement of the Sheriff Courts (Scotland) Act 1971 might competently be brought in the sheriff's small debt court or were required to be brought in the summary manner used under the Small Debt Acts.[8]

---

[4] Sheriff Courts (Civil Jurisdiction and Procedure) (Scotland) Act 1963.
[5] Grant Committee, p.188.
[6] s.35, as amended by SI No. 842 and the Act of Sederunt (Summary Cause Rules, Sheriff Court) 1976 (SI 1976 No. 476). And most recently the Act of Sederunt (Summary Cause) Rules 2002 (SSI 2002/132).
[7] Sheriff Courts (Scotland) Act 1971 (Privative Jurisdiction and Summary Cause) Order 1988 (SI 1988 No. 1993).
[8] Sheriff Courts (Scotland) Act 1971, s.35(1).

Summary cause was not and is not what is now meant by a small claims procedure, for that term refers not simply to a judicial procedure dealing with claims below a certain figure. The important features of a small claims procedure are cheapness to litigants, simplicity of procedure, speedy and efficient disposal of cases, and impartial adjudication. While summary cause is less complex than traditional sheriff court procedure it by no means meets these criteria. The Hughes Report[9] accepted that there was considerable evidence to show that it is too expensive and too complex. Some idea of its complexity may be gauged from the fact that the rules setting out the procedure and its forms extended to some 50 pages and were drafted in a way which makes it all too plain that laymen were never intended to read them.[10] The complexity of the procedures deters potential litigants and makes expensive professional legal assistance virtually essential to bring a case. Given the uncertainty of litigation, the fact that a successful litigant can recover at least some of his expenses from his opponent is not sufficient to dispel fears based on grounds of expense. Empirical evidence in a Scottish Office report underlines this problem: "in the small proportion of cases that went to proof, if expenses were awarded these were high (up to several hundred pounds), and this caused a good deal of concern to the people involved in the case."[11]

The summary cause procedure is not without its merits as the Hughes Report observed. "The summary cause serves a useful purpose in disposing of routine cases of undisputed debt". In the context of the creation of a small claims procedure it is the remainder of this sentence which is important for the report goes on to say that "it does not appear to encourage individuals to pursue claims—either individual claims for debt or consumer and other claims."[12]

Given this situation, it is not surprising that the Scottish Consumer Council, on its formation in 1975, soon identified the creation of a small claims procedure as an important priority.[13] The Council set up a working party to look at procedures which had been adopted in other jurisdictions and to consider if, and how, such procedures might be

---

[9] *Report of the Royal Commission on Legal Services in Scotland*, Cmnd. 7846 (1980).

[10] I.D. Macphail, "The role of the Sheriff Court in Providing a Cheap, Quick and Simple Procedure" in *Report on Small Claims Seminar*, pp.14–28, Glasgow, Scottish Consumer Council, 1978. The current version (see Act of Sederunt (Summary Cause) Rules 2002 (SSI 2002/132)) runs to 155 pages but is much better drafted.

[11] *A Research Based Evaluation of the Dundee Small Claims Experiment*, para. 6.13, Scottish Office, Central Research Unit (1983).

[12] Hughes Report, pp.175–176.

[13] See M.G. Clarke, *Consumer Law in Scotland—A Discussion Document*, Glasgow, Scottish Consumer Council, 1976.

introduced into the Scottish system.[14] The working party proposed the setting-up of an experimental small claims scheme modelled, to some extent, on those then operating in Manchester and Westminster, if financial backing could be arranged. This plan was overtaken by the announcement by the Lord Advocate of his intention to introduce on an experimental basis at Dundee Sheriff Court, a small claims adjudication scheme as part of a wider ranging review of summary cause.[15]

While the introduction of the experimental scheme owed much to the efforts of the Scottish Consumer Council's working party, it is worth placing it, and the new small claims procedure itself, in a wider context. It may be said they are the Scottish response to a general phenomenon which owes its origin to a movement begun in the United States in 1913 with the publication of an article by Dean Roscoe Pound[16] and the establishment in Cleveland of a conciliation branch of the Municipal Court. These events led to the introduction of a variety of different schemes in the United States and other common law jurisdictions. It was not until the late 1960s that the issue was taken up in the United Kingdom[17] and as recently as 1973 that an arbitration scheme was introduced into the county courts in England and Wales,[18] and 1979 in Northern Ireland.[19] The attention drawn to the need for improved redress procedures for consumers in the European Community's first consumer protection programme and the Hilkens Report[20] also provided a valuable support for those in Scotland who were advocating the introduction of proper small claims procedures. At a practical level, the Commission's assistance and the evident interest of its consumer protection service were important in launching an experimental scheme.

The Dundee scheme operated from 1979 to 1981 and was a voluntary scheme in that both parties had to agree to participate. Cases could be brought where sums of money up to £500 were claimed. It had simple

---

[14] The working party was chaired by Mr Matthew Clarke, then a lecturer in law at the University of Edinburgh, and comprised a sheriff, two experienced court practitioners nominated by the Law Society of Scotland, the director of Consumer Protection in Fife, a solicitor, the secretary of Glasgow Chamber of Commerce, and a Citizens' Advice Bureau worker.

[15] Written answer, H.C.Parl.Deb. (5th series), 957 col.198.

[16] "The Administration of Justice in the Modern City" (1913) 26 *Harvard Law Review*, 302.

[17] See *Justice Out of Reach*, Consumer Council, London, 1970, H.M.S.O.

[18] See G. Appelby, "Small Claims in England and Wales," in M. Capalleti and B. Garth (eds), *Access to Justice*, Vol.II, pp.683–763, Milan, Sijthoff & Noordhoff, 1978.

[19] *Report of the Royal Commission on Legal Services in Scotland*, Cmnd. 7846 (1980).

[20] *Study of the Section for Protection of the Environment, Public Health, and Consumer Affairs on the use of Judicial and Quasi Judicial Means of Consumer Protection in the European Community and their Harmonisation*, Brussels, 1979, European Economic and Social Committee.

rules written in plain English and running to less than three typescript pages. Adjudication was by the sheriffs based in Dundee, and in reaching a settlement they had wide discretion about the methods to be used. Legal representation was not prohibited and a party could be represented by someone other than a solicitor. Almost all parties represented themselves, a practice which the rules about expenses were designed to encourage. Expenses could be awarded against a party subject to a maximum of £25, a sum which would not cover a high proportion of a solicitor's fee. There was no provision for an appeal.

The scheme received 52 claims. The largest group of claims, 34, involved consumer disputes and of these 18 concerned complaints about faulty goods and 16 unsatisfactory services. Of the other categories 10 could be described as debt recovery action and there were six delictual claims mostly involving personal injury actions. There were 13 hearings under the scheme and in a further five cases the defender admitted the claim, three making full payment and two offering a lower sum in settlement. At first sight the number of claims and hearings would appear to be disappointing. However, it must be remembered that this was a voluntary scheme designed to test court procedures not an attempt to assess demand for a new procedure. The official report on the scheme stated that in research terms the experiment was a success in that it "was possible to conduct a full examination of the way in which the small claims scheme operated at Dundee Sheriff Court" and that the experiment showed that simplified procedures for dealing with small claims could work effectively in the sheriff court.[21]

While the Dundee experiment was in progress the report of the Hughes Commission recommended "that there should be a small claims procedure within the sheriff court which is sufficiently simple, cheap, quick and informal to encourage individual litigants to use it themselves without legal representation.[22]

Section 18 of the Law Reform (Miscellaneous Provisions) (Scotland) Act 1985 provided the enabling legislation for the creation of the small claims procedure. That section effected amendments of the Sheriff Courts (Scotland) Act 1971 but it did not provide full details of the new procedure. To see the full picture it is necessary, in addition, to look at subordinate legislation. The Small Claims (Scotland) Order 1988 (SI 1988/1999) made by the Lord Advocate, defines what a small claim is and sets the financial limits relating to expenses. The Act of Sederunt (Small Claims Rules) 1988 (SI 1988/1976) contained the rules of the

[21] *A Research Based Evaluation of the Dundee Small Claims Experiment*, Scottish Office, Central Research Unit, 1983.
[22] Hughes, para.11.21.

original scheme drawn up by the Sheriff Court Rules Council. For the sake of completeness it is worth noting that another order, the Sheriff Courts (Scotland) Act 1971 (Privative Jurisdiction and Summary Cause Order) 1988 (SI 1988/1993), increases the privative jurisdiction of the sheriff court and the upper limit for conventional summary cause to £1,500.

The procedure was the subject of a major research project involving researchers from the Central Research Unit of the Scottish Office and academics from the universities of Dundee and Strathclyde. The report, *Small Claims in the Sheriff Court in Scotland: An assessment of the use and operation of the procedure*,[23] found that the vast majority of claims were payment actions, mostly debt collection actions. The procedure was quick but claimants and their representatives were often critical of the hearings which rarely seemed to be conducted with much informality. Preliminary hearings were sometimes not conducted in accordance with the rules which prescribed that the sheriff should identify the disputed issues. Sheriffs were universally praised for the fairness of their decisions and court staff were warmly praised for their helpfulness.

A later research study looked at the impact of small claim procedure on personal injury litigation.[24] This study found that the procedure had made an impact on low value personal injury claims which extended beyond those within the small claim limit, and that unrepresented litigants found it difficult to assess the value of their claims and cope with the procedure. The study also reinforced the finding of the CRU study that informality was often lacking in the procedure.

The views of commentators on the procedure have varied. The present writer argued that while not an unqualified success, it had achieved some modest gains in making the courts accessible to lay people.[25] Others have taken a quite different view.[26]

The new rules follow a lengthy period of consultation during which the Sheriff Court Rules Council issued a consultation paper[27] and the Scottish Courts Administration produced a consultation paper on raising the financial limits for Sheriff Court procedures.[28] The new rules were

---

[23] Central Research Unit, Scottish Office, Edinburgh, 1991.

[24] E. Samuel, *In the Shadow of the Small Claims Court: The Impact of Small Claims Procedure on personal Injury Litigants and Litigation* (Scottish Office, Edinburgh, 1998).

[25] Ervine, "Small Claims: A Progress Report", 1992 S.L.T. (News) 33.

[26] D. O'Carroll and P. Brown, "Small Claims: An Abject Failure and a Threat to Legal Aid?" (1991) 182 SCOLAG 154.

[27] *A Consultation on Proposed New Rules for Summary Cause and Small Claim Procedure in the Sheriff Court* (Scottish Courts Administration, Edinburgh, 1998).

[28] *Proposals to Increase Jurisdiction Limits in the Sheriff Court (including privative jurisdiction limit)* (Scottish Courts Administration, Edinburgh, 1998).

finally brought into force on June 10, 2002. It was expected that the financial limits would be increased at the same time but this has not happened. The Scottish legal system, therefore, basks in the luxury of two procedures for claims for up to £1,500.[29]

These rules are analysed in detail in the following chapters. They contain some useful innovations. Unlike the previous rules, they provide a complete set of rules for small claims. No longer are rules incorporated from summary cause and ordinary cause procedure. A serious effort has been made to express the rules in clear English and the drafting has been modernised. An interesting innovation is the inclusion in Appendix 2 of a glossary explaining technical terms which cannot be avoided. This is included in the Act of Sederunt containing the rules but it is made clear in rule 1.1(5) that it has no significance for the purposes of interpretation.

---

[29] For some stimulating comments on reform see N.M.P. Morrison, *Reform of Civil Procedure*, 1998 S.L.T. (News) 137.

CHAPTER 2

DEFINITION OF A SMALL CLAIM

The kinds of action which may be brought as small claims are limited. The starting point in defining what is a small claim is s.35(2) of the Sheriff Courts (Scotland) Act 1971 which was substituted for the original subsection by s.18(1) of the Law Reform (Miscellaneous Provisions) (Scotland) Act 1985. Section 35(2) states:

> "(2) There shall be a form of summary cause process, to be known as a 'small claim,' which shall be used for the purposes of such descriptions of summary cause proceedings as are prescribed by the Lord Advocate by order."

This immediately limits the range of cases which can be brought as small claims because s.35(1) of the Sheriff Courts (Scotland) Act 1971 sets out a limited range of actions which must be brought as summary causes. To discover exactly which types of action can be brought as small claims it is necessary to consider not only the primary legislation but also the Small Claims (Scotland) Order 1988 [1] The effect of art.2 of the Order and s.37(2C) of the Act is that small claims comprise the following three types of action:

(i) actions for payment of money not exceeding £750 in amount (exclusive of interest and expenses) other than actions in respect of aliment and interim aliment and actions of defamation;

(ii) actions *ad factum praestandum* and actions for the recovery of possession of moveable property where in any such action there is included, as an alternative to the claim, a claim for payment of a sum not exceeding £750 (exclusive of interest and expenses); and

---

[1] SI 1988/1999.

9

(iii) actions in categories (i) and (ii) which are excluded only because
       of the monetary limits if the parties agree.

PAYMENT ACTIONS

As was the case with the original summary cause procedure so with the
small claims procedure the most common type of action has been the
payment action. Actions of aliment and interim aliment are excluded
from the small claims procedure as are actions of defamation; and the
category of small claims payment actions is further reduced by the
financial restriction.

The most common type of payment action is what is commonly
referred to as a debt action. The pursuer, often a finance house, mail
order company or public utility sues for sums due under a contract. The
vast majority of these actions are undefended and the small claims
procedure has taken on the role of a debt collection procedure.

However, debt actions are not the only types of contractual action to
come before the small claims court. Where the amount claimed is less
than £750 small claims procedure must be used for other contractual
actions where a sum of money is claimed. These can take various forms.
Where, for example, the purchaser of goods contends that the goods are
defective his claim under the Sale of Goods Act 1979 that one of the
implied terms about quality has been breached will be competent as a
small claim. The claim will either be for damages for breach of contract
or, where the goods have been rejected, for the purchase price together
also, in appropriate cases, with damages. If the purchaser has not paid
for the goods then what might otherwise look like a debt action brought
by the supplier of the goods may well become a disputed case in which
the purchaser defends the action on the same basis.

Another contractual action for payment which seems to have arisen
not infrequently as a small claim has related to building or home
improvement work. The defender is a customer who refuses to pay any
or all of a tradesman's bill because of dissatisfaction with the quality of
the work done. The claim arises as a payment action and is defended on
the ground that the full sum is not due because of a failure to meet the
standard of quality implied by law that the work should be done in a
proper and workmanlike manner. Depending on the circumstances, it
may be that the customer has to take the initiative and sue for damages
for breach of contract.

In addition to contractual actions some of the more common types of
payment action arise from situations that legally are classified as delictual. As will be noted below there has been a good deal of controversy

about the suitability of the small claims procedure for dealing with personal injury actions. There is, however, no doubt that such actions are competent as small claims payment actions. Some arise from injuries at work as the reported case of *Robertson v D.B. Marshall (Newbridge) Ltd*[2] demonstrates, or from minor car accidents. Another circumstance in which car accidents may give rise to small claims payment actions is where a driver has been reimbursed by an insurer for most of the damage suffered in an accident but wishes to recover from the other driver any excess which is not recoverable under the policy.

The amount of the claim may have to be considered in some cases where there is a question whether it should be raised as a small claim or as a summary cause.[3] The financial limit is £750 *"exclusive of interest and expenses"*. This phrase is discussed in the chapter on Jurisdiction.[4]

ACTIONS *AD FACTUM PRAESTANDUM* AND ACTIONS FOR THE RECOVERY OF MOVEABLES

As we have seen, actions *ad factum praestandum* can be brought as small claims provided that there is included as an alternative to the claim a claim for payment of a sum not exceeding £750 (exclusive of interest and expenses). In *The Law of Civil Remedies in Scotland* Professor Walker defines an action *ad factum praestandum* as follows:

> "A Decree *ad factum praestandum* is a judicial order to do or perform some act, other than to pay money, which the defender should have done in implement of a legal duty incumbent on him, whether by statute, common law or by contractual undertaking, or an order to undo some act which the defender should not have done but did in breach of a legal duty incumbent on him."[5]

There is some imprecision about the scope of the action which probably explains why, in art.3 of the Small Claims (Scotland) Order 1988, it is stated that for the purposes of defining small claims "actions *ad factum praestandum* include actions for delivery and actions for implement but do not include actions for count, reckoning and payment." The exclusion of actions for count, reckoning and payment is justified because

---

[2] 1989 S.L.T. (Sh.Ct.) 102.
[3] It will also be relevant in relation to expenses.
[4] See pp.16 and 17.
[5] See p.269.

they tend to be complex and thus not suitable for a procedure intended to deal fairly informally with relatively straightforward cases.

This category covers a wide range of actions. In practice, it is most often invoked by television rental companies wishing to recover their property from errant customers. It was used in a small claims action at Dunfermline Sheriff Court to recover a garden ornament which was in the possession of a person not entitled to it.[6] Another example might involve a request for the return of goods deposited for repair. It would, as a request for a decree of specific implement, be the action to raise where it was sought to require the other party to a contract to fulfil his obligations under it.[7] In relation to small claims it might be used in this context to require a tradesman to complete a job which he had started but was tardy in completing.

This type of small claim is unlikely to be much used in non-consumer contracts for the sale of goods. It is true that there is a presumption in Scots law that an obligation is enforceable by a decree of specific implement unless to do so would be inequitable. In practice it will be rare for a contract for the sale of goods to be enforced in this way. This is because it will usually be possible to obtain goods from another source and damages will almost always be a satisfactory remedy. It will only be where the goods are unique that a decree of specific implement will be an appropriate remedy.[8]

However, the additional rights of a buyer in consumer cases set out in the new Part 5A of the Sale of Goods Act 1979, and the new Part 1B of the Supply of Goods and Services Act 1982 may increase the number of these claims. These provisions were introduced by the Supply of Goods to Consumers Regulations 2002 which implement the E.C. Directive on Sale of Goods and Associated Guarantees.[8a] As a result, in certain circumstances buyers of goods have a right to a repair or replacement if goods are defective.

The inclusion of the alternative money claim is to provide a means of segregating those claims suitable for small claims from those involving more valuable assets. As Professor Walker points out in his book on *Civil Remedies*[9] the defender does not have the option of meeting the money claim. Should the defender fail to obey the order of the court the pursuer may, of course, choose to accept damages but he may attempt

---

[6] See the Dundee *Courier* April 15, 1989.
[7] See *McKellar v Dallas's Ltd*, 1928 S.C. 503.
[8] Walker, *Law of Civil Remedies in Scotland*, p.276.
[8a] Directive 1999/44/EC O.J. No. L 171, 7.7.99, p.12. See Ervine, 2003 S.L.T. (News) 67.
[9] *ibid.* p.282.

to enforce implement. The main sanction for failure to carry out the order is imprisonment, which cannot be for more than six months, and may be brought to an end earlier if the defender complies with the original decree.[10] Imprisonment does not extinguish the obligation to comply with the order. The court may substitute such money payment as seems just and equitable; or, if the decree was to deliver corporeal moveables, give warrant to officers of court to search, take possession and deliver up any moveables found.[11] In *Ford v Bell Chandler*[12] it was held that an application under the Act was competent even where those against whom it was sought were outside the jurisdiction of the sheriff court and could not have been subject to imprisonment. In such a case the alternative of a money payment will be ordered.

SMALL CLAIMS BY AGREEMENT

This category of small claims is that referred to at (iii) above at p.10. Strictly speaking it is not a separate type of action. Section 37(2C) of the Sheriff Courts (Scotland) Act 1971 gives the parties to a dispute involving a sum in excess of the current upper limit for small claims of £750 the option of resolving it under the least formal sheriff court procedure. However, both parties must agree. If they do so the case is then treated for all purposes like any other small claim. This means, for example, that the special rules about representation and expenses apply to it as well as the limitations on appeal.

An example of a situation where use might be made of this provision might be the following problem over the purchase of a used car. A person purchases a second-hand car from a garage for £4,000 and within a very short time it proves to be seriously defective. The purchaser rejects the car, to use the language of the Sale of Goods Act 1979, and requests the return of the purchase price and possibly damages for inconvenience and the hiring of a replacement car. The garage does not comply and it is clear that the dispute will have to be resolved in the courts. This action would be a form of payment action, but because it is for more than £750 it does not automatically qualify to be brought as a small claim. However, if both purchaser and garage agree and make a joint motion to the sheriff he must direct that the cause shall be treated as a small claim.

[10] Law Reform (Miscellaneous Provisions) (Scotland) Act 1940, s.1(1)(a).
[11] *ibid.*, s.1(2) and *United Dominions Trust (Commercial) Ltd v Hayes*, 1966 S.L.T. (Sh.Ct.) 101.
[12] 1977 S.L.T. (Sh.Ct.) 90.

It does not appear that any use has been made of this provision. The logic of this provision is that there is no necessary link between the value of a dispute and its legal or factual complexity. The advantages of using it are that the dispute can be resolved in the sheriff court in a relatively informal manner which has built into it protections against exposure to excessive expense. In practice, tactical considerations may well come into play where the possibility of using this facility arises. There is no incentive for a legally aided person to use it; and the opponent of someone who is not legally aided might well refuse to collaborate in the hope that fear of the expense involved in summary cause or ordinary actions might result in a settlement more advantageous to him or her. The most obvious situation in which the facility could have attractions might be where both parties are private individuals who are prepared to represent themselves.

EXCLUDED ACTIONS

We have already seen that there are some exceptions to the types of action otherwise competent as small claims. In addition, an action which on the face of it falls within the definition of a small claim already discussed may not be dealt with under that procedure. Under s.37(2B)(b) of the Sheriff Courts (Scotland) Act 1971, the sheriff must remit a small claim to the conventional summary cause roll or the ordinary roll if the parties present a joint motion to that effect. It is understood that this was used under the original rules where the defender wished to make a counterclaim for which there was no provision. It might well be used where it is obvious that the dispute involves complex facts or difficult points of law more suitable for more sophisticated procedures.

In addition, the sheriff has power under s.37(2B)(a) of the Sheriff Courts (Scotland) Act 1971, either of his own motion or on the motion of one of the parties, to remit to the conventional summary cause or ordinary rolls. This he may do "if he is of the opinion that a difficult question of law or a question of fact of exceptional complexity is involved". The sheriff's decision is not subject to review.[13] It is not thought that this power has been exercised much by sheriffs either of their own motion or on the motion of one of the parties. In *Robertson v D.B. Marshall (Newbridge) Ltd*[14] Sheriff Macphail referred to the tests

---

[13] Sheriff Courts (Scotland) Act 1971, s.37(3)(a).
[14] *Supra*, n.2.

in a personal injuries case. The action had been raised as a conventional summary cause although the solicitors for the pursuer knew that the value of the claim did not exceed the small claim limit. This they did to attempt to obtain expenses on the summary cause scale rather than being limited by the expenses rules applicable to small claims. Having refused to award expenses on the summary cause scale the learned sheriff discussed whether if the action had been raised as a small claim he would have directed that it be treated as a summary cause under s.37(2B)(a) of the Sheriff Courts (Scotland) Act 1971. He stated that he would not have done so. Referring to the grounds for doing so he said:

> "These are stiff tests, and I am not persuaded that any such questions are involved in this case. The nature of the accident and the grounds of liability are commonplace, and the invocation of s.8 of the Administration of Justice Act 1982 does not appear to raise any such question as is referred to in subs. (2B)(a).
>
> "I accept, of course, that the case was too difficult for the pursuer to present adequately without legal representation, and that an award of £75 will not cover her legal expenses. I cannot, however, bend the rules by condoning the raising as a summary cause of an action which clearly fell within the description of a small claim."

In *Gorham v G.B. Papers Ltd*[15] Sheriff Principal R. R. Taylor agreed with Sheriff MacPhail's judgment and observed that the appeal related to "a simple run of the mill reparation action" which there would have been no reason to remit had it been raised as a small claim.

For more guidance on the application of this test assistance may be sought from a case considering the slightly different test applicable to remits from summary cause to ordinary cause, or ordinary cause to the Court of Session. That test is that the sheriff "is of the opinion that the importance or difficulty of the cause makes it appropriate to do so." In *Butler v Thom*[16] Sheriff MacPhail observed:

> " '[T]he difficulty of the cause' would appear not to be limited to the 'complexity of the matters at issue,' which might give rise to difficulty in decision, but to include difficulty in procedure, preparation or presentation: as where a defender reasonably seeks to employ third-party procedure ... ; or where a party reasonably

[15] Feb. 10, 1990.
[16] 1982 S.L.T. (Sh.Ct.) 57.

seeks to adduce the oral evidence of a witness furth of Scotland, who cannot be compelled to attend the sheriff court. 'The difficulty of the cause' is, however, a criterion different from and stricter than that of expediency, which justifies the transfer of a cause to another sheriff court on grounds of convenience."[17]

[17] *ibid.*, p.58.

CHAPTER 3

JURISDICTION

In dealing with litigation it is always important to consider the issue of jurisdiction. To use the definition of Sheriff Macphail in *Sheriff Court Practice*:

"The 'jurisdiction' of a validity constituted court connotes the limits which are imposed upon its power to try a cause and pronounce therein valid and enforceable decrees, by reference to three considerations: (1) the subject-matter of the cause, in that the court must have power to deal with it; (2) the remedy which is sought or the application which is made, in that the court must have power to grant it and the proceedings must conform to the practice and procedure of the court as to the way in which it will exercise its power to do so; and (3) the persons convened as defenders or the conduct or property in respect of which the remedy is desired or the application is made, in that the court must in general have authority over such persons or conduct or property."[1]

The topic of jurisdiction is a large and complicated one and it is not proposed to deal with it in detail here. Discussion will be limited to those aspects of the topic which are particularly relevant in the context of small claims procedure.[2]

SUBJECT-MATTER OF THE CAUSE

The first aspect of jurisdiction is the issue of the subject-matter of the cause. In this respect, small claims is a narrow jurisdiction as the legislation creating the procedure restricts it in two ways. This is in addition to the fact that, as a species of summary cause, it is already

---

[1] Macphail (2nd ed.), Vol.1, para.2.01.
[2] See Macphail and also Anton, *Civil Jurisdiction in Scotland.*

limited by the fact that it could not be greater than the existing jurisdiction of the sheriff court to entertain summary cause actions. Only two types of action are competent: payment actions; and actions *ad factum praestandum* and actions for the recovery of moveable property as defined by the Small Claims (Scotland) Order 1988, arts.2 and 3. In addition, the same order imposes a financial limit on the small claims jurisdiction.[3]

Where, as in small claims actions, jurisdiction is in part determined by financial limits, problems are likely to arise on the amount of the claim. In relation to actions *ad factum praestandum* the problem does not arise, as the Small Claims (Scotland) Order makes clear that there must be an alternative crave of a sum not exceeding £750 exclusive of interest and expenses.

In payment actions the Order (like s.35 of the Sheriff Courts (Scotland) Act 1971) makes clear that the amount of the claim excludes interest and expenses. The excluded interest is not only interest from the date of citation but all interest which is merely an accessory of the principal sum sued for. As Sheriff Macphail observes,[4] it is not clear whether interest which is treated as part of and included in the principal sum sued for should be excluded. *Bowie v Donaldson*[5] is not clear on this point. Lord Salvesen agrees that in "certain cases, the only conclusion in the summons may be for a certain sum or arrears of interest under an obligation the principal of which has already been satisfied. In that case the sum sued for is the principal sum, it is not an accessory; and, although it may be due in respect of arrears of interest, it does not cease to be the principal sum sued for."[6] The learned judge does not directly answer the question raised where the claim is for a mixture of principal and interest. The logic of his judgment would seem to be that in this situation the criterion for valuing the claim should be the amount of the principal sum.

Generally speaking the value of the cause is the sum sued for. However there may be circumstances where this rule will be displaced if the sum claimed does not represent the true value of the cause. There is a series of cases cited in Macphail, of which *Scottish Special Housing Association v Maxwell*[7] is an example, to support this point.[8] There, what was ostensibly a claim for arrears of rent raised what was really a test case governing a number of claims. It seems likely that the same

---

[3] Discussed in chapter on "Definition of a Small Claim".
[4] Macphail (2nd ed.), Vol.1, paras 2.27–2.34.
[5] 1922 S.C. 9.
[6] *ibid.* at 13.
[7] 1960 S.C. 391.
[8] Macphail, para.2.29 and footnotes thereto.

principle would apply in relation to small claims. In such circumstances it might in any event be a suitable case for remission to another roll on the grounds of complexity.

PERSONS AND PROPERTY

The third aspect of jurisdiction, the persons who may be convened as defenders or the property in respect of which of pursuer seeks a remedy, is governed mainly by the Civil Jurisdiction and Judgments Act 1982. Professor Black has referred to the advantages of having a "mind similar to that necessary (or desirable) in masters of the game of three dimensional chess"[9] when grappling with this Act and this is not the place to unravel its mysteries. In any event, given the relatively narrow range of actions which are competent as small claims there are many aspects of the jurisdiction rules which are not relevant. Brief reference is made to the main rules about this aspect of jurisdiction, but the reader is referred to Sheriff MacPhail's *Sheriff Court Practice* for a fuller treatment.

The Civil Jurisdiction and Judgments Act 1982 was passed to incorporate into U.K. law the terms of the 1968 Brussels Convention on Jurisdiction and the Enforcement of Judgments in Civil and Commercial Matters.[10] That, *inter alia*, dealt with jurisdiction issues between Member States. The opportunity was also taken, in effect, to apply the same principles to issues of jurisdiction arising between the three law districts in the United Kingdom, and the allocation of jurisdiction between sheriffdoms. The transnational rules were found in Schedule 1 to the Act, the *intra* UK rules in Schedule 4 and the Scottish rules in Schedule 8.

The Convention has recently been replaced by the Brussels Regulation.[11] As this is an EC Regulation it is directly applicable in all Member States, except Denmark which is still subject to the Convention. The Civil Jurisdiction and Judgments 2001[12] amends the 1982 Act by substituting, with effect from March 1, 2002, this Regulation for the convention in Schedule 1 to the Act. In line with the policy of applying the same rules to *intra* UK and Scottish jurisdiction issues the Order makes changes in Schedules 4 and 8 of the Act.

---

[9] Black, *Civil Jurisdiction—the new rules: a guide for the perplexed.*
[10] O.J. No. L304, 30.10.1978, p.36.
[11] Council Regulation (EC) No. 44/2001 O.J. L 12/1, 16.1.2001.
[12] SI 2001/3929.

States not party to the Brussels Regulation are subject to the Lugano
Convention of 1988 which is in similar terms to the Brussels Regulations. It was given effect to by the Civil Jurisdiction and Judgments Act
1991.

The basic approach

Whether the jurisdiction issue is one between member states, different
parts of the United Kingdom or sheriffdoms within Scotland the general
approach of the Act is the same. As Schedule 8, rule 1, applying to
jurisdiction within Scotland puts it, "Subject to the following rules,
persons shall be sued in the courts for the place where they are domiciled". Schedule 4, rule 1 provides that "persons domiciled in a part of
the United Kingdom shall be sued in the courts of that part", and Article
2 of the Regulation states that "Subject to this Regulation persons
domiciled in a Member State shall, whatever their nationality, be sued
in the courts of that Member State".

Domicile for this purpose in the case of individuals means that the
person is resident in the United Kingdom, Scotland or the particular
sheriffdom depending on the particular situation and that he has a
substantial connection with the relevant area. A person is taken to be
resident if he has been resident in an area for the last three months or
more; and is deemed to have a substantial connection unless the contrary is proved.[13]

Corporations and associations are domiciled where they have their
"seat". They have their seats in the United Kingdom if incorporated or
formed under the law of a part of the United Kingdom and have their
registered office or some other official address in the United Kingdom,
and their central management and control is exercised in the United
Kingdom. A corporation or association will be domiciled in Scotland if
(a) it has its seat or some other official address in Scotland, or its central
management and control is exercised in Scotland, or it has a place of
business there. The corporation or association may be sued in the
sheriffdom in which the places referred to in (b) above are situated.[14]

Exceptions

To the general principle that the courts of the domicile of the defender
have jurisdiction there are certain qualifications of which only those

---

[13] Civil Jurisdiction and Judgments Act 1982, s.41.
[14] *ibid.*, ss.42 and 43.

which are most likely to be relevant to small claims actions will be discussed. In certain circumstances a court other than that of the defender's domicile may have concurrent jurisdiction. This may occur in relation to contract, delict or a dispute arising out of the operations of a branch, agency or other establishment. In relation to the allocation of jurisdiction within Scotland these rules are to be found in rule 2 of Schedule 8 of the Act which is entitled *Special Jurisdiction.*

Contract exception

The first special rule relates to contract and provides that the defender may also be sued in the courts of the place of performance of the obligation. Like the equivalent rules in Schedule 4[15] and the Brussels Regulation,[16] this is subject to the rules relating to consumer contracts discussed below. There is an example here of not following the general policy of aligning the rules in the Brussels Regulation and the domestic rules in Schedules 4 and 8. The Brussels Regulation expands on the meaning of "place of performance" in relation to contracts for the sale of goods and contracts for services. It provides that a contract for the sale of goods, unless otherwise agreed, is performed in "the place in a Member State where, under the contract, the goods were delivered or should have been delivered". In the case of contracts for services the place is that where the "services were provided or should have been provided". These additions to the original rule in the Brussels Convention have not been included in the Schedules 4 and 8. The reason is that it is thought likely that the new provision will generate a significant amount of uncertainty at least in the period immediately after its commencement.

Delict

In delictual or quasi-delictual matters there is concurrent jurisdiction with the courts of the "place where the harmful event occurred". In *Handelskwekerij G.H. Bier B.V. v Mines de Potasse d'Alsace S.A.*[17] it was held that this expression included both the place where the damage was suffered and the place where the act which have rise to the damage was performed.

[15] Sch.4, r.3.
[16] Art.5(1).
[17] [1976] E.C.R. 1735.

Operation of a branch or agency

A person may also be sued in courts other than those of the state or area where he or she is domiciled if the dispute arose out of the operations of a branch or agency. In this case the courts of the place in which the branch or agency are situated have concurrent jurisdiction. Again, as with contractual claims, this rules is subject to the special rules about consumer contracts.[18]

Consumer contracts

As indicated in the previous paragraphs, there are special rules about jurisdiction which favour consumers and can be of considerable benefit to them tactically. These apply, to quote rule 3.1 of Schedule 8, to certain "matters relating to a contract concluded by a person, the consumer, for a purpose which can be regarded as being outside his trade or profession".[19] In these cases the consumer may choose to make a claim in the courts of the place where he or she is domiciled as well as the courts of the domicile of the defender. Three types of consumer contract are affected. The first two are contracts for the sale of goods on instalment credit terms and contracts for a loan repayable by instalments, or for any other form of credit, made to finance the sale of goods. The third type is:

> "in all other cases, the contract has been concluded with a person who pursues commercial or professional activities in Scotland or, by any means, directs such activities to Scotland or to several places including Scotland, and the contract falls within the scope of such activities."

This provision contains one of the few amendments brought about by the Brussels Regulation. The original version applied where the conclusion of the contract was preceded by a specific invitation addressed to the consumer or by advertising. The amendment is considerably wider than the original provision and was, in part, designed with the expansion of various means of cross-border trading such as the Internet in mind. While it may well be Internet sales that are likely to be the paradigm example for the use of this provision it should be noted that it is wide enough to cover other situations. The Department of Trade and Industry

---

[18] Sch.8, r.2(f); Sch.2, r.3(e); and Brussels Regulation, Art.5(5).
[19] This is in the same terms as Art.15(1) of the Brussels Regulation and r.7.1 of Sch.4.

guidance note[20] suggests, for example, that a UK consumer who buys goods while on holiday in France would be able to sue in a UK court if the trader (who would not necessarily be French) had pursued or by any means directed his activities to the UK.

Internet sellers have been exercised about the width of this provision fearing that they could be exposed to actions in jurisdictions in which they had never intended to do business. This will turn on whether it can be said that the seller "directs such activities to that Member State or to several Member States including that Member State". To try to allay concern on this issue the EC Council and Commission issued a joint statement[21] pointing out "that it is not sufficient for an undertaking to target its activities at the Member State of the consumer's residence . . . a contract must also be concluded within the framework of its activities". It goes on to stress "that the mere fact that an Internet site is accessible is not sufficient for [the provision] to be applicable, although a factor will be that this Internet site solicits the conclusion of distance contracts and that a contract has actually been concluded at a distance, by whatever means". Contrary to the DTI guidance note the joint statement says that the currency and language of a website are not relevant.

To avail themselves of the advantages conferred on consumers the contract must be "for a purpose which can be regarded as outside his trade or profession". The word "outside" is significant as the sheriff in *Semple Fraser v Quayle*[22] appreciated. The defenders who was sued by a firm of solicitors for professional fees incurred in proceedings concerning his disqualification as a company directors argued that he was being sued in his capacity as a consumer. If this was correct he could be sued only in England where he was resident, not in Scotland. The sheriff held that the correct test was that set out in the judgment of the European Court of Justice in *Benincasa v Dentalkit Srl*,[23] which he stated as follows:

"The test is whether the purpose of the contract is to satisfy the individual needs in terms of private consumption of the person being supplied with the goods and services. If the contract is connected or related to the trade or profession of the party in receipt of the goods or services then it cannot be said that the 'consumer' is acting outside his trade or profession. Accordingly

---

[20] *www.dti.gov.uk/ccp/topics1/guide/jurisdiction_htm*
[21] Most easily found via a link in the DTI website referred to above.
[22] 2002 S.L.T. (Sh.Ct) 33.
[23] C269/95; [1997] E.C.R. I–3767; [1998] All E.R. (EC) 135.

the 'consumer' in such a contract is not entitled to the protection afforded by rule 3."[24]

As the Advocate General stated in his opinion,[25] "Although [what is now Article 15] aims to protect the weaker party in a contractual relationship, its scope is limited to contracts in which one party is acting for purposes unrelated to a business activity, that is to say as a 'private final consumer not engaged in trade or professional activities'". He went on to add that "the mere fact that one of the parties to a contract concluded with a view to the pursuit of a trade or professional activity or in the course of such activities is in an inferior position, as in the case of franchise agreements, is not regarded by the Brussels Convention [now the Brussels Regulation] as requiring special protection in relation to the attribution of jurisdiction."[26]

In deciding that the defender was not a consumer for the purposes of the special jurisdiction rules the sheriff refused to follow the decision of Sheriff Principal McLeod in *J Mann (Advertising) Ltd v ACE Welding and Fabrications Ltd*.[27] In this it is submitted that he was correct as that decision is clearly inconsistent with the decision in *Benincasa*. The issue also arose in *Lynch v Bradley*,[28] another case of a solicitor suing for professional fees. This case is not necessarily wrongly decided as it is not clear from the report what the nature of the services rendered to the client were.

The special consumer rules do not apply to a transport contract unless it is one "which, for an inclusive price, provides for a combination of travel and accommodation".[29] This usefully makes clear that package holiday contracts are not contracts of transport. Insurance contracts are not subject to the special contract rules at least where the Brussels Regulation applies or there is concurrent jurisdiction between Scotland and another part of the United Kingdom.[30]

The jurisdiction rules relating to consumer contracts can be departed from only by agreement between the parties made after the dispute has arisen or where the agreement extends the number of courts in which an action can be raised.[31]

---

[24] 2002 S.L.T. (Sh.Ct.) 33 at 37.
[25] *op. cit.* n.23, para.51.
[26] *ibid.*, para.52.
[27] 1994 S.C.L.R. 763.
[28] 1993 S.L.T. (Sh.Ct.) 2.
[29] See Sch.8, r.2(3)(2), Sch.4, r.7(2) and Brussels Regulation, Art.15(3).
[30] Brussels Regulation, s.3 and Sch.4, r.7(2). It seems that the special protection does apply where there is concurrent jurisdiction between sheriffdoms.
[31] Brussels Regulation, Art.17, Sch.4, r.9 and Sch.8, r.3(6).

PROROGATION OF JURISDICTION

It is not uncommon in standard form contracts and other commercial contracts to find a clause providing that the courts of a particular part of the United Kingdom or some other country will have jurisdiction. This is an example of prorogation of jurisdiction. Where the parties are bargaining on an equal footing there is nothing objectionable. Where they are not, as is typically the case in consumer contracts, there may be unfairness. It is for this reason, as has been noted in the previous paragraph, that in relation to consumer contracts there is limited scope for the parties to vary the jurisdiction rules.

In some other circumstances this is also possible. The three Schedules to the Act dealing with the various potential jurisdictional choices have similar rules on this matter. An agreement conferring jurisdiction must be in writing or evidenced in writing. Where the parties have agreed that the courts of a particular state, or law district, or sheriffdom are to settle any disputes which arise, the court chosen has exclusive jurisdiction.

SUBMISSION TO JURISDICTION

Should a defender enter an appearance before a court in response to a small claim that court shall have jurisdiction. To confer jurisdiction in these circumstances it is not enough that an appearance has been entered solely to contest the jurisdiction. Merely to intimate an intention to appear by completing the appropriate form of response as provided by rule 9.1(1) indicating that a challenge to the jurisdiction of the court does not amount to a submission to jurisdiction.

PLEADING A GROUND OF JURISDICTION

Rule 4.2 of the Small Claim Rules does not require the statement of claim to set out a ground of jurisdiction, no doubt for the reason that Sheriff Principal MacLeod gave in his judgment in *British Gas plc v Darling*[32] that "It is not to be expected that a pursuer in small claims procedure will know the rules governing jurisdiction or even be aware of the concept of jurisdiction." As he pointed out, the rules leave it to the

[32] 1990 S.L.T. (Sh.Ct.) 53.

sheriff clerk or the sheriff to glean from the statement of claim and other parts of the summons whether there is a ground of jurisdiction. In many cases this will be obvious. In the *British Gas* case the Sheriff Principal considered that, in deciding for the purposes of issuing a summons, it was only necessary to disclose, prima facie, that there was a ground of jurisdiction and that it was enough that the pursuer was described as residing at an address within the jurisdiction of the court.

Where one of the less common grounds of jurisdiction is relied on it would be wise to set this out in the summons. For example, where the consumer contract qualification to the basic rule is relied on it is useful to do this. There have been some examples of summonses not being issued by sheriff clerks where this ground of jurisdiction was relied on but not stated on the summons. In any event rule 21.1 provides that the sheriff must not grant a decree against a defender (or a pursuer on a counterclaim) "unless satisfied that a ground of jurisdiction exists."

CHAPTER 4

RAISING THE ACTION

Having established that the action that it is proposed to raise is competent as a small claim and that the sheriff court has jurisdiction, the action
may be raised. In this chapter the raising of the action and the responses
to it are described. The payment action is described in detail, as the
overwhelming majority of small claims fall into this category. In the
new rules, unlike the original set, the payment action and those for
delivery, recovery of possession of moveable property and implement of
an action are not dealt with in separate parts. Where the nature of the
latter actions requires a different approach to that of the payment action
this is dealt with at the appropriate point.

The detailed rules concerning the raising and prosecution of a small
claim are contained in the Schedule to the Act of Sederunt (Small
Claims Rules) 2002,[1] which came into force on June 10, 2002. A
valuable improvement in the presentation of these rules as compared
with their predecessors is that they contain all the rules relating to small
claims. No longer does one have to make reference to a list of summary
cause and ordinary cause rules which apply to a small claim.

There has been some difference of opinion on the correct approach to
interpreting and applying the rules of the small claims procedure. In
British Gas plc v Darling[2] Sheriff Principal MacLeod observed that
"whether the pursuer is one with an enormous volume of small claims
business or one who raises only one small claims summons in a lifetime,
the approach of the courts must, in my view, be universally liberal and
enabling", and he criticized the "literal and restrictive interpretation" of
the sheriff whose judgment was under appeal. In *North of Scotland
Hydroelectric Board v Braeside Builders Trustees*[3] Sheriff Principal
Hay dissented in part from this approach. He said:

> "While I support in principle the proposition that the court should
> be prepared to adopt a liberal and enabling approach in the small
> claims procedure, I respectfully dissent from the proposition that

[1] SSI 2002/133.
[2] 1990 S.L.T. (Sh.Ct.) 53.
[3] 1990 S.L.T. (Sh.Ct.) 84.

this approach should be universally applied. In my opinion, different considerations may apply where a party is represented by skilled advisers and where one party is an unrepresented party litigant. I do not consider that a liberal and enabling approach should be universally adopted so as to excuse insufficient identification of the disputed issues by solicitors or other skilled advisers. Nor do I consider that the fact that any particular pursuer has a large volume of claims should be an excuse for error."

Sheriff Principal Hay's approach is substantially the traditional approach of the courts to the party litigant.[4] In so far as he is criticising Sheriff Principal MacLeod for condoning the use of slipshod methods by solicitors his comments may be somewhat harsh. It is perfectly possible to see Sheriff Principal MacLeod's remarks as recognising the greater informality of small claims and perhaps going a little further than a sheriff might be expected to go under the more traditional procedures where it has been said that his objective "is to attain the ascertainment of the truth and the doing of justice, and not to give scope for encouragement to tactical manoeuvring."[5]

THE PAYMENT ACTION

Rule 4.1 provides that a small claim shall be commenced by summons in Form 1 of the forms set out in Appendix 1 to the rules. The defender's copy will vary depending on the nature of the claim. Where it is for, or includes, payment of money and a time to pay direction or time order may be applied for Form 1a should be used. In all other cases the appropriate Form is 1b. The summons must be "authenticated by the sheriff clerk in some appropriate manner" to quote rule 4.4. The original rule had referred to the summons being "signed" and the change has been made to anticipate the possibility of dealing with a summons electronically in the future. If, for some reason the sheriff clerk refuses to authenticate the summons or the defender's address is unknown or the pursuer seeks to alter the normal period of notice rule 4.4(2) provides that the sheriff shall authenticate it if he thinks it appropriate. Rule 4.4(3) provides that, when signed, the summons is warrant for service on the defender and, where the appropriate warrant has been

---

[4] See Macphail (2nd ed.), Vol.1, paras 4–118 to 4–120.
[5] Macphail (2nd ed.), Vol.1, para.16.38. See also the comments of Sheriff Principal Bowen in *Scott v Chief Constable of Strathclyde*, 1999 S.L.T. (Sh.Ct.) 66.

included in the summons, warrant for arrestment on the dependence or for arrestment to found jurisdiction.

As with other procedures in the sheriff court, persons carrying on business under a trading or descriptive name may sue and be sued in that name.[6]

Until s.32 of the Solicitors (Scotland) Act 1980 was amended by the Law Reform (Miscellaneous Provisions) (Scotland) Act 1990 there had been some uncertainty about the ability of employees or officers of corporations such as limited companies to draft a small claim summons. Such doubts have been removed by Sch.8, para.29. It amends s.32 of the Solicitors (Scotland) Act 1980, which makes it an offence for unqualified persons to prepare certain documents, in two ways. Section 32(1)(b), which prohibits the preparation of documents relating to legal proceedings, does not apply to anyone who is permitted to represent a party to a summary cause of which, it is to be remembered, a small claim is a species. As an employee or officer of a corporation could be an authorised lay representative of the kind permitted by rule 2 to represent a party they come within the scope of s.32(1)(b). In addition, the exemption from liability in s.32(2)(a) for those acting without "fee, gain or reward" has been extended to those acting "other than by way of remuneration paid under a contract of employment". Small Claim Rule 2.1.2 reflects this situation by providing that "An authorised lay representative may in representing a party do everything for the preparation and conduct of a small claim as may be done by an individual conducting his own claim".

THE STATEMENT OF CLAIM

The primary requirement of the statement of claim as set out in rule 4.2 is that it should "give the defender fair notice of the claim." The rule goes on to list more specific requirements. The statement of claim must set out "details of the basis of the small claim including relevant dates." Where the claim arises from the supply of goods or services, details of the goods or services and the date or dates on or between which they were ordered and supplied must be included.

Unlike the original rules there is no requirement in the new rules to refer to any agreement which gives another court jurisdiction over the subject-matter of the claim, or that there are proceedings pending before

[6] r.6.1.

another court involving the same cause of action and the same parties.

It is to be noted that the small claims rules do not require the pursuer to refer to a ground of jurisdiction. For the reasons given in the chapter on jurisdiction, it can be desirable to do so, especially where this is not patently obvious from the summons.

As has been noted above, in *British Gas plc v Darling*,[7] Sheriff Principal MacLeod was prepared to tolerate "shorthand methods" in completing the statement of claim because "the approach of the courts must, in my view the universally liberal and enabling in this procedure." He regarded as complying with the rules a statement of claim which consisted of a copy of the statement of account for work done for the defender on a stated date together with an assertion that the defender had failed to pay the account. Although the statement of claim did not state the precise date on which goods and services were ordered the Sheriff Principal took the view that this was of no practical importance in this case. It was clear when, approximately, they had been ordered and that this "prima facie satisfies the demands of fair notice". This general approach did not commend itself to Sheriff Principal Hay.[8] It is not clear, however, whether he would have regarded the specific practice under review in that case as complying with the rule about statements of claim.

In an earlier part of his judgment Sheriff Principal Hay appears to agree with the view of the sheriff in the case under appeal that the statement of claim should set out the basis in law of the small claim. Rule 4.2(a) (like the original rule 3(4)(a) with which the Sheriff Principal was concerned) refers to "details of the basis of the small claim". It does not explicitly say that the pursuer must set out the *legal* basis of his claim. If the rule is to be interpreted in this way it will make it very difficult for litigants in person to use the procedure. It may be that the sheriff meant only that the facts disclosed in the statement of claim should set out a relevant cause of action. Certainly, it would be odd if more than that were necessary in view of the fact, as Sheriff MacPhail observes, in his *Sheriff Court Practice*,[9] that in conventional summary cause procedure "it should be noted that there is *prima facie* no requirement for a statement of claim to give any indication of the legal basis for the claim; only a concise statement of facts need be given." In small claim procedure this is underlined by the rule on the function of the

---

[7] See note 1 above.
[8] *North of Scotland Hydro-Electric Board v Braeside Builders Trs*, 1990 S.L.T. 84.
[9] Macphail (2nd ed.), Vol.1, p.814, para.25–20.

Hearing (rule 9.2) which states that one of the functions of that hearing is to ascertain the legal basis of the claim.[10]

In *Mannifield v Douglas Walker*[11] Sheriff Principal Nicholson seems to have accepted this view in a small claim where the statement of claim was drafted and the case presented by a lay litigant. He warned of the problems that this could present:

> "I daresay that, in many instances where a small claims is pre-sented by a lay person, there will be no difficulty in ascertaining the legal principle which is being invoked in support of it. In other cases, however, that will not be so and in that event I think the sheriff who hears such a case must take great care to establish what, if any, legal principle is an issue, particularly if, as here, the sheriff decides to proceed by way of an informal investigation of the circumstances rather than by way of the formal leading of evidence."

As has been noted, the overriding requirement of the statement of claim is that it should give the defender fair notice of the claim. There have been no decisions on this phrase so far in appeals on small claims but the similar provision in the summary cause rules has been commented on in a number of cases referred to in *Sheriff Court Practice*.[12] Sheriff MacInnes observed in *Bird's Eye Foods Limited v Johnston*[13] that "the test must be whether from reading a statement of claim and any documents referred to therein, copies of which are attached to the summons, the defender is given fair notice of the claim which is being made against him." As Sheriff Principal Walker pointed out in *South of Scotland Electricity Board v Frazher*,[14] a case under the old summary cause procedure: "it seems to me undesirable that any person should deliberately raise an action in such a way as to give no indication to the defender or to the court of the basis of the claim." However, "Elaborate pleadings are out of place in a summary cause, but it seems to me that the rules call for each party to give to the other the minimum notice, albeit in a few words, of what he hopes to prove."[15] Sheriff Principal Caplan's observation must surely be as true of small claims as the procedure it related to:

---

[10] See discussion in Chap.5.
[11] 1990 S.C.L.R. 369.
[12] See Macphail (2nd ed.), Vol.1, p.815 and relevant footnotes.
[13] Cupar Sheriff Court, Feb. 3, 1977, unreported.
[14] Glasgow Sheriff Court, Feb. 7, 1974, unreported.
[15] Sheriff Principal O'Brien in *Bennett v Livingston Development Corporation*, Linlithgow Sh.Ct., Oct 29, 1979, unreported.

> "the summary cause pleader does not require to present a case which can pass a relevancy test prior to proof. He only requires to give reasonable notice of his case and he ought also to bear in mind that it is in the essential nature of the summary cause procedure that the defender may not be legally represented."[16]

Indeed, one might add to that last comment that the judiciary should bear in mind that in small claims procedure not only may the defender not be legally represented, the statement of claim may have been drafted by the pursuer himself without professional assistance.

Rule 9.2, dealing with the purpose of what is referred to as "the Hearing", should be borne in mind. This Hearing takes the place of the preliminary hearing under the original rules. One of the purposes of this hearing is that the sheriff shall "ascertain the factual basis of the claim and any defence, and the legal basis on which the claim and defence are proceeding".[17] The same rule goes on to require the sheriff, where it is not possible to settle the dispute, to identify and note on the summons the agreed and disputed facts and the issues of law which are in dispute. This implies that something considerably less than precision in drafting the statement of claim is expected.

NOTICE AND RETURN DATE

Rule 4.5 provides that the small claim shall proceed after the appropriate period of notice has been given to the defender. Where the defender is resident or has a place of business within Europe that period is 21 days; where resident outwith Europe, 42 days.[18] Where a period of notice expires on a Saturday, Sunday, public or local holiday, the period of notice shall be deemed to expire on the first following day on which the sheriff clerk's office is open for civil business. Where service of a summons is by post, the period of notice shall start to run from the day after the day of posting.[19]

The sheriff clerk inserts in the summons the date of the last day of the notice period. This is known as the "return day" and is the last date on which the defender my return a response form to the sheriff clerk. He or

---

[16] *Visionhire Ltd v Dick*, Kilmarnock Sheriff Court, Sept. 18, 1984, unreported.
[17] r.9.2.2.
[18] r.4.5(3).
[19] r.4.5(5).

she also inserts in the summons the date set for the hearing of the claim which is referred to as "the hearing date".[20]

SERVICE

The defender has a known address in Scotland

Where the address of the defender is known and is in Scotland, rule 5 deals with the method of service. Where the defender is resident in Scotland a service copy summons shall be served on the defender by the pursuer's solicitor, a sheriff officer or the sheriff clerk sending it by first class recorded delivery post.[21] This is the normal method and only if this proves not to be possible will one of the other methods specified in rule 6.1(3)(b) or 6.4 be used. These involve a sheriff officer citing the defender either by tendering the summons to the defender personally or by the leaving it in the hands of an inmate at the defender's dwelling place or with an employee at the defender's place of business.[22] Only if these methods fail may the sheriff officer, "after making diligent inquiries" serve the summons by either depositing it in the defender's dwelling place or place of business by letter box or other lawful means or by affixing it to the door of the defender's dwelling place or place of business.[23] Where either of these methods is used the sheriff officer must then send by ordinary post a letter containing a copy of the summons to the address at which he thinks it is most likely that the defender may be found.[24] The sheriff officer may be an officer of either the court which granted the summons or of the sheriff court district in which it is to be executed. It is not necessary for the sheriff clerk of the defender's residence to endorse the summons.[25]

Where the pursuer is neither a partnership nor a body corporate nor acting in a representative capacity, s.36A of the Sheriff Courts (Scotland) Act 1971 provides that he may require the sheriff clerk to serve the summons on his behalf. This provision is one of the features of the small claims procedure designed to encourage individuals to use it. The reference to persons acting in a representative capacity would apply to executors, trustees and curators bonis. Where the sheriff clerk effects service he may do so by recorded delivery post

[20] r.4.5(6).
[21] r.6.3(1).
[22] r.6.4.
[23] r.6.4(2).
[24] r.6.4(3).
[25] r.6.7.

or, on payment to him by the pursuer of the appropriate fee, by sheriff officer.[26]

The outside of the envelope containing the service copy summons must contain a statement indicating that it contains a notice from the sheriff court and a form of service in Form 5 must be enclosed with the service copy summons.[27]

Defender has a known address outside Scotland

Where the defender lives outwith Scotland service is effected as provided in rule 6.5. Where the defender lives in the United Kingdom, the Isle of Man, the Channel Islands or any country with which the United Kingdom does not have a convention providing for service of writs in that country, service may be either in accordance with the rules for personal service under the law of that place or by registered or recorded delivery post in Scotland.[28]

In many cases there are international treaties governing service of documents abroad. The two most important are the Hague Convention on the Service Abroad of Judicial and Extra-Judicial Documents in Civil or Commercial Matters dated November 15, 1965[29] and the European Convention on Jurisdiction and Enforcement of Judgments in Civil and Commercial Matters usually referred to as the Brussels Convention. Where the document has to be served in a country which is party to one of these conventions rule 6.5(3) requires service to be effected in one of the five ways set out in them. These are:

(a) by a method prescribed by the internal law of the country where service is to be effected for the service of documents in domestic actions upon persons who are within its territory;

(b) by or through a British consular authority at the request of the Secretary of State for Foreign and Commonwealth Affairs;

(c) by or through a central authority in the country where service is to be effected at the request of the Secretary of State for Foreign and Commonwealth Affairs;

(d) where the law of the country in which the person resides permits, by posting in Scotland a copy of the document in a registered letter addressed to the person at his residence; or

[26] r.6.4(6).
[27] r.6.2(1).
[28] r.6.5.3.
[29] Cmnd. 3986 (1969).

(e) where the law of the country in which service is to be effected permits, service by an *huissier*, other judicial officer or competent official of the country where service is to be made.

If the document requires to be served in a country to which Council Regulation (EC) No.1348/2000 on the service in the Member States of judicial and extrajudicial documents in civil or commercial matters applies, service may be effected by a method prescribed in paragraph (3)(b) or (c) only in exceptional circumstances.[30]

Where methods (b) or (c) are used, rule 6.5(8) provides that a copy of the summons and warrant for service with form of service attached must be sent to the Secretary of State for Foreign and Commonwealth Affairs indicating the method of service. When the summons has been served the pursuer must lodge in process a certificate of execution of service signed by the authority which has effected service.[31]

Where method (e) is used and the services an *huissier* have been employed, the pursuer must send to that official a copy of the summons and warrant for service, with citation attached, or other document, with a request for service to be effected by delivery to the defender or his residence. When service has been effected the pursuer must lodge in process a certificate of execution of service by the official who has effected it.

Where the document has to be served in a country other than those referred to in rule 6.5.3 with which the United Kingdom has a convention on service of writs the methods approved in the relevant convention must be used.[32]

The address of the defender is not known
Where the address of the defender is not known the method of service is governed by rule 6.6. It will be recalled that by virtue of rule 4.4 this is one of the cases where the summons must be authenticated by the sheriff rather than the sheriff clerk. Service will either be by an advertisement in a newspaper circulating in the area of the defender's last known address or by displaying a notice (as set out to in Form 8) on the walls of the court, usually referred to as "walling". The period of notice, which is to be fixed by the sheriff, runs from the date of the publication of the advertisement for the display of the notice on the walls of the

[30] r.6.5(4).
[31] r.6.5(8).
[32] r.6.5(5).

court. The pursuer lodges a service copy summons with the sheriff clerk from whom it may be uplifted by the defender. Under rule 6.6(5), a personal pursuer, who is entitled to require the sheriff clerk to effect service, bears the cost of the advertisement and must pay the cost to the sheriff clerk before he instructs the publication of the advertisement.

Should the address of the defender become known after service has been effected by an advertisement or walling, rule 6.6(8) provides that the sheriff may allow the summons to be amended to and, if appropriate, grant warrant for re-service subject to such conditions as he thinks fit.

Re-service
Rule 6.9 deals with re-service. If it appears that there has been any failure or irregularity in service the court may prior to, or at, the hearing and, upon such conditions as seem just, authorise the pursuer to re-serve the summons and thereafter that claim proceeds as if it were a new claim.

Return of the summons
If someone other than the sheriff clerk has served the summons and the case requires to call in court on the hearing date the pursuer must return the summons and the certificate of execution of service to the sheriff clerk at least two days before the hearing date.[33] If the case does not require to call in court the pursuer need only return the certificate of execution of service to the sheriff clerk at least two days before the hearing date.[34] Failure to observe these requirements will lead to the sheriff dismissing the claim.[35]

Where the sheriff clerk has served the summons, which an individual can require him or her to do, it is up to the pursuer to find out from the sheriff clerk's office what response has been received. The sheriff clerk is no longer obliged, as was the case under the original rule 7(2), to inform him or her.

Contents of the envelope in which the summons is served
The original rules provided that nothing could be included in the envelope containing a defender's copy summons which did not form

[33] r.6.11(1).
[34] r.6.11(2).
[35] r.6.11(3).

part of the summons, a response or other notice. The sensible rationale for this was that nothing should be included with the summons that might distract attention from this important document. This might have been the case if commercial promotional or advertising material had been included. The rule, however, prevented helpful, explanatory material being included. For example, it prevented information about the valuable Edinburgh in court advice scheme being included. The new version of the rule provides a limited exception to the ban on additional material. It is now possible to include any other document approved by the Sheriff Principal.[36]

DEFENDER'S RESPONSES

There are five possible responses which the defender may make on receiving the summons.

(i) The claim may be admitted and payment in full made together with expenses and interest. The pursuer's solicitor will then ask for the claim to be dismissed. Should he or she not do so the small claim would automatically be dismissed by virtue of rule 8.1(4).

(ii) The defender may make no response. In this case rule 8.1 provides that the claim will not call in court. The pursuer should lodge a minute in form 11 requesting the court to grant decree. This must be done before the sheriff clerk's office closes for business on the second day before the hearing date. Decree will usually be granted in these circumstances though, as with grant of any decree, the sheriff must be satisfied that a ground of jurisdiction exists. Failure to lodge a minute leads to dismissal of the claim. Lateness in minuting for decree in this way could be cured by the dispensing power of the sheriff contained in rule 3.1.

There can be circumstances where the pursuer does not immediately wish to seek decree. It may be that a cheque from the defender has still to clear or, as in *Jenner's Princes Street Edinburgh Limited v McPherson*,[37] that full details of expenses are not available. In that case the pursuer had entered a minute "to call please". This was not considered appropriate: it is essential that

---

[36] r.6.8.
[37] 1992 S.L.T. (Sh.Ct.) 18.

the minute should clearly state what the pursuer wants the court to do.

(iii) Some defenders may respond in terms of rule 8.2(1) by admitting the claim and making written application for a time to pay direction or a time order. The time to pay direction is an order under the Debtors (Scotland) Act 1987 requesting that a sum owed be paid by instalments or in a lump sum but at a later date. Time orders are similar orders governed by the Consumer Credit Act 1974. A recall or restriction of an arrestment may be coupled with such an application. The defender in this case is not intending to appear at the Hearing. As a time to pay direction under the Debtors (Scotland) Act 1987 is being requested only individual defenders, as opposed to corporations, may make this response. It is done by completing and returning the appropriate parts of Form 2. Box 1 of that form must be signed and section B completed. Section B sets out the terms of the time to pay direction requested and has a questionnaire about income, outgoings and dependants which the defender should fill in. This response must be lodged with the sheriff clerk on or before the return date.

If the pursuer agrees to the defender's proposals there is no need for the case to call in court. The pursuer intimates acceptance by lodging a minute in Form 12 before the sheriff clerk's office closes for business on the day occurring two days before the hearing date and seeking decree.[38] On the hearing date the sheriff grants decree.[39]

If the pursuer does not accept the defender's proposals, a minute in Form 13 to that effect should be lodged with the sheriff clerk by the close of business two days before the hearing date.[40] The case calls in court on the hearing date and the sheriff decides the application and grants decree.[41]

(iv) The fourth response is similar to the third except that, while admitting that claim, the defender attends the Hearing to make an application for a time to pay a direction. Rule 8.2(1) provides that the defender should indicate his or her intention by completing the appropriate part of the form of response (box 2 of section B) attached to the service copy summons and lodge with the sheriff clerk on or before the return day.

[38] r.8.2(2).
[39] r.8.2(3).
[40] r.8.2(4).
[41] r.8.2(5).

(v) Like the previous response, the fifth group of responses involves the defender in indicating an intention to appear at the Hearing, and these are governed by a rule 9.1. In all these cases the defender must indicate an intention by completing the appropriate part of the response (box 3 of Form 1a or 1b) attached to the service copy summons and lodging it with the sheriff clerk on or before the return day.

The first of these situations is fairly rare and occurs where the defender challenges the jurisdiction of the court. It has occurred in one or two cases arising out of package holidays where the defender, a tour operator, no doubt did not wish to be put at a disadvantage by defending in action in the pursuer's sheriff court.

The defender may also indicate that he will appear to defend the small claim or to dispute its amount.[42] The rules set these out as two separate responses. This seems unnecessary as a challenge to the amount claimed is but one kind of defence. It may be that the rule has been drafted in this way to make it clear to lay defenders, who may not seek professional help, that not only may they dispute liability but also admit liability and dispute the amount for which they are liable.

ACTIONS FOR DELIVERY

The original rules had special provisions in Part III for actions for delivery etc. While the procedure was largely the same as for payment actions there were some differences, notably that there was no return day. The new rules do not have a part dealing specifically with these cases and they proceed in the same manner as payment actions.

COUNTERCLAIMS

The original rules did not include the facility to make a counterclaim, as it was thought inappropriate in a simplified procedure.[43] In practice, situations arose where a defender had a counterclaim and some sheriffs

---

[42] r.9.1(b) and (c).
[43] See *Jenners of Edinburgh v Norris*, 2001 S.C.L.R. 516, where the defender not only resisted the claim but attempted to lodge a counterclaim for $100 million.

found a way to resolve what were two separate claims as efficiently as possible, as *Slessor-Burnett v Stuart*[44] demonstrates. The consultation exercises carried out by the Rules Council demonstrated that there was support for the provision of a counterclaim and this is now provided in Chapter 2 of the new rules.

Where defenders intend to make counterclaims they must indicate their intention on the form of response. It is not necessary to do more, as the substance of the counterclaim need only be divulged orally at the hearing. It would seem to be in the interests of defenders to do more than this, and state the nature of the counterclaim in writing on the form of response. This is likely to expedite the resolution of the case as the pursuer will be more likely to be in a position to respond to the counterclaim at the hearing. Indeed, Rule 11.1(5) anticipates this by providing that " . . . the sheriff may continue the Hearing to allow an answer to the counterclaim to be stated". The case may also be unnecessarily prolonged by failure to state a counterclaim in writing where the pursuer has failed to appear or be represented at the hearing. Rule 11.1(7) provides that in this situation the sheriff may continue the hearing after noting the counterclaim and the factual basis of it to allow the pursuer to appear. The sheriff clerk informs the pursuer of this hearing using form 14 and advises him or her that failure to appear or be represented may result in a decree against them being granted in terms of the counterclaim. Form 14 appears to provide for no more than a bare warning that a counterclaim has been stated and of the consequences for the pursuer of failing to appear at the continued hearing. How the pursuer discovers the substance of the counterclaim is not clear as the defender is under no obligation to inform him or her.

The defender may not only indicate on the response form an intention to state a counterclaim but may also set out the substance of that claim.[45] If this path is chosen the defender must send a copy of the response form to the pursuer and any other party to the claim.[46] Booklet 3 of the Scottish Court Service's series of information booklets *Responding to a Small Claim*, helpfully provides a specimen counterclaim.

If the written counterclaim seeks warrant for arrestment on the dependence or arrestment to found jurisdiction, the sheriff clerk may authenticate it[47] or the defender may apply at the hearing for it to be authenticated.[48] The authenticated warrant then becomes warrant for

---

[44] 1990 S.L.T. (Sh.Ct.) 62.
[45] r.11.1(1)(b)(i).
[46] r.11.1(2).
[47] r.11.1(3)(a).
[48] r.11.1(3)(c).

arrestment or arrestment to found jurisdiction as the case may be.[49] Should the sheriff clerk, when requested to authenticate the counter-claim, refuse to do so, then, as with authentication of the summons, the Sheriff may do so.[50]

A counterclaim will normally be stated at or before the Hearing. Rule 11.1(6) provides that a counterclaim may be stated after the Hearing or any continuation of it only with a leave of the Sheriff. It seems unlikely that this should arise if the Hearing is conducted as envisaged in Chapter 9 of the rules.

THIRD PARTY PROCEDURE

Small claims procedure has no provision for third-party procedure. Where it might be wished to invoke such procedure an incidental application to remit to summary cause or ordinary cause would be necessary and, probably, successful.

[49] r.11.3.
[50] r.11.1(4).

CHAPTER 5

HEARINGS

The small claims procedure can involve six types of hearing: a Hearing; a hearing on a time to pay application or time order in an undefended claim where the pursuer has not accepted the defender's written proposals or the defender wishes to make a proposal in court; a hearing on evidence; a hearing on a minute for recall of a decree; a hearing of an incidental application; and an appeal.

THE HEARING

Where the claim is defended Chapter 9 of the rules provides that it shall go to "the Hearing".[1] The capital letter is important and distinguishes this type of hearing from the others. The Hearing is clearly intended to be the most significant type of hearing. It occurs where defenders have indicated on the response part of Form 1a or 1b that they intend to challenge the jurisdiction of the court, state a defence (which can include a counterclaim), or dispute the amount of the claim,[2] The Hearing is held on the hearing date which is seven days after the return day,[3] and If the dispute is not resolved on that day the sheriff has power to continue the Hearing until another appropriate day.[4]

Rule 9.1(5) provides that the defender must appear or be represented at the Hearing and should he or she fail to appear or be represented, and the pursuer does appear, decree may be granted against the defender.[5] This is subject to the over-riding requirement that the sheriff is satisfied that there is a ground of jurisdiction.[6] Should the defender appear but the pursuer fail to turn up or be represented the claim may be dismissed.[7] If all the parties fail to appear the sheriff will normally dismiss

[1] r.9.1(2).
[2] r.9.1(1).
[3] r.9.1(3).
[4] r.9.1(4).
[5] r.9.1(6).
[6] r.21.1.
[7] r.9.1(7).

the claim.[8] It may transpire at the Hearing that there is no legal basis for the pursuer's claim or that there is a patent defect of jurisdiction. Rule 9.2(1) provides that, in these circumstances, the sheriff must dismiss the claim or, if another sheriff court would have jurisdiction, he or she may exercise the power in rule 15.1(2) to transfer it to the appropriate court.

The purpose of the Hearing

Where the parties appear or are represented and there is a substantive issue between them the rules give guidance on the purpose and conduct of the Hearing. The starting point is rule 9.1(5) which directs the sheriff to "note any challenge, defence or dispute, as the case may be, on the summons". Unlike the original rules there is no explicit reference to the possibility of a written defence having been submitted in advance of the Hearing. The submission of a written defence with the response form or separately could be helpful in resolving the dispute more expeditiously.[9] The expectation in the rules seems to be that the defence will be stated at the Hearing.

One of the major criticisms of the original small claim procedure was that preliminary hearings (as they were then termed) were not always being conducted as intended or, indeed, as directed by the rules.

The Scottish Office research report found that while all sheriffs interviewed noted the defence not all of them went on to discover the issues in dispute as the then rules required.[10] This is borne out in judgments in small claims appeals where it is clear that some of the difficulties stemmed from a failure to ascertain the disputed issue properly.[11] It is not surprising that the same research project revealed that few disputed cases were resolved at that stage, although the rules encouraged the sheriff to effect a settlement at that point.

The new rules expand on the guidance in the original rules in a way which leaves no room for doubt about the purpose of the Hearing. Rule 9.2 is entitled "Purpose of the Hearing" and directs the sheriff to:

---

[8] r.9.1(8).
[9] For a case which demonstrated that there could be dangers in doing this see *Scott v Chief Constable of Strathclyde* 1999 S.L.T. (Sh.Ct.) 66.
[10] *Small Claims in the Sheriff Court in Scotland*, Scottish Office, Central Research Unit Papers, Edinburgh (1991), p.79.
[11] See *North of Scotland Hydro-Electric Board v Braeside Builders' Trs*, 1990 S.L.T. (Sh. Ct.) 84. *Kostric v O'Hara*, 1990 S.C.L.R. 129 and *Mannifield v Walker*, 1990 S.C.L.R. 369.

"(a) ascertain the factual basis of the claim and any defence, and the legal basis on which the claim and defence are proceeding; and

(b) seek to negotiate and secure settlement of the claim between the parties."[12]

This clearly indicates a more interventionist role for sheriffs than many have been prepared to contemplate in the past. Particularly where lay litigants are involved it will require the "more inquisitorial attitude on the part of the Sheriff" which Sheriff Principal Ireland considered the original rules envisaged.[13] It is no great novelty and, indeed, only spells out in the rules what one Sheriff Principal considered the correct approach under the original rules. Sheriff Principal Nicholson observed:

"Unfortunately, I think that the absence of any clear indication of the legal basis of the respondent's claim has probably led to many of the difficulties which have arisen here. I dare say that, in many instances where a small claim is presented by a lay person, there will be no difficulty in ascertaining the legal principle which is being invoked in support of it. In other cases, however, that will not be so and in that event I think that a sheriff who hears such a case must take great care to establish what, if any, legal principle is in issue."[14]

This part of rule 9 and the later requirement to identify and note the disputed issues is designed, as Sheriff Principal Nicholson said of the equivalent provisions of the original rules, "to impose some sort of structure on a small claim hearing by identifying those matters which are in issue".[15]

It will not only be cases involving lay persons that will require this approach. As the Scottish Office research noted, there was a tendency under the old rules, especially where both sides were legally represented, for some sheriffs to treat a small claim in the same manner as a traditional summary cause. As some appeal judgments show, where the issues were not properly defined in the pleadings this was the cause of difficulties at a later stage. Proper attention to the rules ought to ensure that this does not happen under the new regime. A further advantage is that it might dispose of some claims at this point. Establishing clearly

---

[12] r.9.2(2).
[13] *Slessor v Burnett-Stuart*, 1990 S.L.T. (Sh.Ct.) 62.
[14] *Mannifield v Walker*, 1990 S.C.L.R. 369.
[15] *Kuklinski v Hassell*, 1993 S.L.T. (Sh.Ct.) 23.

what the bases of the claim and defence are might, on some occasions, reveal that there is no valid legal claim or defence.

It hardly needs saying that it is essential that the defender states a proper defence. In *Hamilton v Ansah*[16] the Sheriff Principal emphasised the importance of this in rejecting the argument that the assertion "debt denied" constituted a proper defence. In that case the pursuer had raised an action for wages alleged not to have been paid. The pursuer had indicated that he would appear or be represented at the preliminary hearing (as it was known under the original rules) to defend the action. At that hearing his solicitor, who had not been given instructions before the defender had gone abroad, offered "debt denied" as a defence. The Sheriff Principal pointed out that:

> "A pursuer should not have to go to proof on a defence consisting of a bare denial. In such a case as this she would not know whether the appellant was disputing that she had been at work on the days in question, that she was entitled to sick leave and pay for annual leave, the rate of pay and number of days claimed by her, or even that she had been in his employment at all."

There was some uncertainty in the approach to ascertaining the basis of the claim under the original rules. In *Slessor v Burnett-Stuart*[17] Sheriff Principal Ireland had observed in the context of a complaint that the sheriff had not properly investigated the basis of the claim that:

> "whatever further steps a sheriff may have to take when dealing with party litigants with no legal knowledge he was not in my view bound to do more than he did in this case, when the parties were represented by solicitors. When he was told that it was admitted that the sum sued for was due, without any mention of a partial defence by way of set off, he was entitled to hold that the facts were sufficiently admitted and to grant decree there and then."

In *North of Scotland Hydro-Electric Board v Braeside Builder's Trustees*, Sheriff Principal Hay referred to this passage and said:

> "I respectfully agree with the proposition that where parties are legally represented the sheriff is under no obligation to explore the disputed issues at the preliminary hearing, and I reject the contrary argument proposed by the pursuers' solicitor."

---

[16] 1990 S.C.L.R. 21.
[17] 1990 S.L.T. (Sh.Ct.) 62.

It is important to note that the Sheriff Principal was rejecting the proposition that the disputed issues should be *explored*, not that they should not be ascertained. It should not be seen as condoning the practice, which seems to have been common under the original rules, of merely accepting the statement of claim and defence proffered by the parties' solicitors. As the late Sheriff Kelbie forcefully pointed out,[18] not only was such a practice not in accordance with the rules but it was also a misreading of what Sheriff Principal Ireland had said.

Having established what the factual and legal bases of the claim and defence (and any counterclaim and response to it) the sheriff is then directed to "seek to negotiate and secure settlement of the claim between the parties". This reflects a desire not only to resolve disputes expeditiously but also to attempt to do so amicably. It also has implications for the organisation of hearings. The sort of arrangements which have been typical of preliminary hearings under the original rules would hardly be conducive to attempts to negotiate a settlement of a claim. Reference is made below in discussing the conduct of hearings to the importance of the physical arrangements for them. It is hard to see how this requirement of the rules can be successfully achieved if more attention is not paid to this aspect of the Hearing.

The duty cast on the sheriff to seek to negotiate and secure settlement of the dispute is a new requirement in the small claim procedure. In practice, under the original procedure it was not unknown for sheriffs to encourage the parties to resolve their disputes even where they had embarked on litigation. The Scottish Office Research Report found that one third of lay advisers had experience of preliminary hearings having been used to encourage settlement.[19] The same report found that some sheriffs had attempted to encourage settlements when the procedure first came in but had been discouraged by their lack of success. Some considered that, having got to court, the parties were not interested in settlement.[20]

Some may feel uncomfortable with this role and perhaps feel that it is somewhat alien to their normal function. This is to overlook the fact that small claim procedure is a novel form intended to resolve claims of small value quickly and cheaply. Although within the traditional court structure it is, in effect, a form of alternative dispute resolution in that it is an alternative to the traditional, purely adversarial, procedures normally employed in the courts. There is, however, a further problem which has been experienced in ADR. This aspect of the small claim

[18] *Small Claims Procedure in the Sheriff Court* (Butterworths, Edinburgh, 1994), para. 6.07.
[19] Research Report, p.63, para.12.
[20] *ibid.*, p.80, para.25.

Hearing raises the difficulty of the same person performing two potentially conflicting roles. In this it resembles the form of ADR known as med/arb (short for mediation/arbitration) which is an amalgam of mediation and arbitration. It has been used by rent officers in England and financial services ombudsmen. Where such a form of ADR is used there is first an attempt to effect a settlement of the dispute by mediation. If this fails the mediator then adopts the role of arbiter and makes a decision. It has been criticised as flawed because it can be argued that, if mediation fails and resort to a decision has to be made, the integrity of the adjudicator's role has been compromised. The arbitrator, or here, the sheriff, may have acquired information in attempting to bring about settlement that should have no bearing on his or her decision as an adjudicator. If mediation fails it will be difficult to block this information out in reaching a decision, and more difficult for the parties to accept that this has been done.[21]

If it does not prove possible to negotiate a settlement the next step is for the sheriff to "identify and note on the summons the issues of fact and law which are in dispute",[22] note on the summons any facts which are agreed[23] and on the basis of this information "reach a decision on the whole dispute".[24] This is similar to rule 13(5) and (6) of the original rules. The drafting of the new rule, however, makes explicit that disputed issues comprise both issues of law and fact. This was a view which was widely accepted under the original rules which referred merely to "disputed issues".[25]

This process, if carried out as intended, may well allow the sheriff to reach a decision on the merits of the case at the Hearing. If, for example, it transpires that there is no difference of opinion between the parties on the facts it may be possible for the sheriff to apply the relevant law and make a decision. Suppose the dispute is between a consumer and a shop about the quality of a product purchased from the shop. It may well be possible to establish that there is no dispute that the product was purchased by the pursuer from the defender. There might also be agreement about the condition of the product. The only issue between the parties is whether the product in that condition meets the statutory term implied by the Sale of Goods Act 1979 that it should be of

---

[21] See L. Fuller, "Collective Bargaining and the Arbitrator", Proceedings, 15th Annual Meeting, National Academy of Arbitrators 8 (1962), quoted in Goldberg, Green and Sander, *Dispute Resolution*, (Little Brown and Co., Boston, 1986).

[22] r.9.2(3)(a).

[23] r.9.2(3)(b).

[24] r.9.2(3)(c).

[25] See *Kostric v O'Hara Car Sales*, 1990 S.C.L.R. 129 and *North of Scotland Hydro-Electric Board v Braeside Builder's Trs*, 1990 S.L.T. (Sh.Ct.) 84.

satisfactory quality. That is a legal issue and a sheriff could there and then make a decision.

It may well be that having established the factual and legal basis of a claim and noted the disputed issues of law there are disputed issues of fact which can only be resolved by having a hearing at which evidence is led. If so, in the final stage of the Hearing the sheriff will "direct parties to lead evidence on the disputed issues of fact which he has noted on the summons",[26] indicate to the parties the matters of fact that require to be proved, and may give guidance on the nature of the evidence to be led.[27] This spells out in more detail what the sheriff should do but it can be seen as declaratory of what has been regarded as good practice.

The original rule 13(5) provided that it was unnecessary for a party to lead evidence on an issue which had not been noted as a disputed issue. Rule 9, the new equivalent of this, does not explicitly say this. The parties will already have conceded certain issues by not challenging them at the Hearing and in addition the sheriff will have directed them on which issues evidence is needed at the evidence on hearing. There is, therefore, no scope for introducing evidence on undisputed issues.

Having conducted the Hearing as directed by rule 9.2 all that remains for the sheriff to do is to fix a "hearing on evidence" for a later date.[28] The purpose and conduct of that hearing is discussed later.

Conduct of hearings

Rule 9.3 deals with the conduct of all types of hearings not just the Hearing, the purpose of which has been discussed above. The overriding requirements are to be found in rule 9.2(2) and (3). Sub paragraph (2) provides that "A hearing shall be conducted as informally as the circumstances of the claim permit" and (3) goes on to state that the:

> "procedure to be adopted shall be such as the sheriff considers—
> (a) to be fair;
> (b) best suited to the clarification and determination of the issues before him; and
> (c) gives each party sufficient opportunity to present his case."

---

[26] r.9.2(4)(a).
[27] r.9.2(4)(b). It would seem that there is now no danger of the problem that arose in *Dunn v David A Hall Ltd*, 1990 S.C.L.R. 673 occurring. See p.53, n.36.
[28] r.9.2(4)(c).

This is similar to rule 19 of the original rules but expands on it slightly. There is no longer any reference to hearings being in public, but with the advent of human rights legislation this is regarded as axiomatic. It might be noted that the requirement to hold hearings in public does not imply that they have to be held in traditional court rooms. The requirement would be met if the venue was one to which the public had access. This is of some importance given the importance of informality. It is not uncommon for hearings to be held in traditional court rooms as one part of the business of the day and no attempt is made to achieve any degree of informality.

Sheriff Principal Nicholson's observation in *Dunn v Hall*[29] about the limits to the conduct of a hearing is still relevant. There he said that the equivalent to rule 9.3(2) to (4) does not:

> "permit a sheriff to decide a case in an injudicial manner, or upon the basis of material which is plainly inadequate to support any kind of decision. For example, a sheriff, in my opinion, would not be entitled to invoke that rule in support of a decision in favour of a party where he had resolved to hear no submissions at all and had decided that the procedure would be that success would go to the party who first addressed him in court. That, of course, is an absurd example but it serves to illustrate that [the rule] does not confer a wholly unfettered discretion on the sheriff."

The conduct of hearings is central to the operation of the small claim procedure and it was an aspect of the original procedure which came in for much criticism, especially from litigants in person and lay advisers. The rules do give sheriffs wide discretion about how they conduct hearings and practice has varied between and within sheriffdoms. In one sheriffdom, for example, it is understood that it is considered impermissible for sheriffs to conduct hearings other than in their normal shrieval dress, whereas some sheriffs in other sheriffdoms have from the beginning of the small claim procedure conducted hearings in everyday dress. In few courts does there seem to be much appreciation of the importance of taking other steps to ensure informality and an atmosphere which will be conducive to reducing the strain for unrepresented litigants for whom this will often be a journey to an unknown land.

The typical scene at preliminary hearings under the original rules certainly was not calculated to put a litigant at ease. A group of black-gowned solicitors sit at the sheriff clerk's table, the unrepresented person is called forward when it is his or her turn and usually stands

---

[29] 1990 S.C.L.R. 673.

behind these lawyers like a suppliant. While the hearing is going on they will often discuss business amongst themselves. Within these constraints sheriffs made attempts with varying degrees of skill to put litigants at their ease and carry on the hearing.

This was bad enough in the context of the preliminary hearing under the original rules. As has been pointed out above, the centre of gravity of the procedure has been tilted more clearly towards what is now called "the Hearing" and the new rules emphasise the purpose of it. If more effective steps are not taken to implement the letter and spirit of the new rules it will be most disappointing and, indeed, it will raise questions whether the requirement of "fairness" is being met. Fairness imports not simply an adjudicator who is impartial and who does not take into account irrelevant considerations in coming to decisions. We have a judiciary with impeccable standards in that respect, and the Scottish Office research found that litigants and their advisers had no quibbles on that score. Fairness imports more than this. To achieve fairness it is necessary to provide a setting in which both parties will feel able to participate. The typical court room scene described in the previous paragraph puts lay litigants at a considerable disadvantage and could hardly be described as fair to them.

Central guidance, perhaps in the form of a practice note agreed by Sheriffs Principal, would be helpful. Such guidance is not unknown in the Scottish court system. A precedent is to be found in the *Memorandum by the Lord Justice General on Child Witnesses*.[30] Some of the suggestions for reducing the stress of a hearing in that context could be applied to small claim procedure. These are: removal of wigs and gowns by the sheriff and solicitors, and having the hearing conducted round a table rather than using the normal court positions.

The other guidelines for conducting the procedure can be seen as aspects of fairness. How they will operate in practice will depend on the circumstances of individual cases. Where both sides are represented by solicitors at a Hearing their implementation should pose fewer problems. They will be accustomed to the venue and to the procedure. At the other extreme is the situation where both sides are unrepresented. This presents considerable difficulties for sheriffs as it requires them to adopt approaches which are very different from those which they are accustomed to use. It is likely that it will be necessary for the sheriff to explain to the parties what the function of the Hearing is. In eliciting the facts and the legal issues it will probably be necessary to adopt an

---

[30] Reproduced in H. Dent and R. Flin (eds), *Children as Witnesses* (John Wiley & Sons, Chichester, 1996).

inquisitorial approach. Lay people cannot be expected to understand what the relevant legal issues are and it will take considerable skill in some cases to tease out from them just what these issues are.

Perhaps the most difficult situation is that where one side is represented by a solicitor and the other is not. The solicitor can be expected to explain the factual and legal side of his or her client's case; the unrepresented litigant cannot. As with the situation where neither side is represented, the sheriff will have to try to ensure that the unrepresented person's case is elicited. The difficulty here is that the sheriff will probably have to probe the unrepresented person's account more deeply than that of the represented person. There is the danger of appearing to favour one side.

While it is not confined to the Hearing, the facility in rule 9.4 for the sheriff to inspect places and objects might be considered at this stage. The rule provides that, where a disputed issue noted by the sheriff is the quality or condition of an object, the sheriff may inspect it in the presence of the parties or their representatives. If it is not practicable to bring the object to court the inspection may take place wherever the object is located. This facility would be useful in some consumer disputes. For example, disputes about "shading" in carpets are common and can be most easily be dealt with by seeing the carpet in question. The legal issue will probably be clear enough in such cases and will usually be: is this product of satisfactory quality? Resolution of the dispute will turn on applying this concept to the facts.

Similarly, the rule permits the sheriff to inspect any place that is material to the disputed issues. Again, this must be done in the presence of the parties or their representative.

A sheriff might not consider that an inspection by him or her would be appropriate but that expert opinion might help to resolve the matter. If the parties agree, the sheriff may, if he considers it appropriate, "remit to any suitable person to report on any matter of fact".[31] This can only be done where the parties have previously agreed the basis upon which the fees of the expert will be paid.[32] From the point of view of the parties this has the advantage of saving expense, in that it saves each side obtaining its own report. If a remit is made and a report is produced that "report shall be final and conclusive with respect to the matter of fact which is the subject of the remit".[33]

---

[31] r.9.5(1).
[32] r.9.5(3).
[33] r.9.5(2).

HEARING WITH EVIDENCE

Where it is not possible to resolve the claim at the Hearing it will be necessary to hold a hearing at which evidence is led. The guidance in rule 9.3 on the conduct of hearings applies to that hearing and some of it is specifically directed to such a hearing.

As with all hearings, a hearing with evidence is to be conducted "as informally as the circumstances of the claim permit".[34] The general guidelines set out in rule 9.3(3) and quoted above also apply. Under the original rules the practice of sheriffs conducting what were then called "full hearings" varied. Sheriff Johnston in an editorial note to the report of *Mannifield v Douglas Walker*[35] observed that "Sheriffs are divided in relation to the approach which should be taken on small claims. One camp advocates an inquisitorial approach while the other prefers the traditional adversarial approach." This variation in practice has itself been a problem as it made it difficult for litigants and their advisers to prepare for hearings not knowing what the likely approach of the sheriff would be. In addition, the procedure adopted might well not have been appropriate to the circumstances of the parties and therefore put one or both of them at a disadvantage.

Under the new rules there is more guidance for sheriffs and a clear indication that, in some circumstances, a departure from an adversarial approach should be adopted. Where both sides are professionally represented it may well be appropriate to conduct the hearing with evidence in the usual adversarial manner. Where one or both parties is unrepresented, the guidance in rule 9.3(3) on fairness and the adoption of a procedure which is best suited to the clarification of the issues and gives both sides a sufficient opportunity to present their cases would point to some departure from conventional practice. Lay persons have no experience of presenting a case by eliciting it from witnesses by examination in chief and challenging an opponent's case by cross examination.

Sub-paragraphs (4) to (6) of the new rules recognise this. Before hearing evidence the sheriff is directed to explain to the parties the form of procedure which he intends to adopt.[36] Sub-paragraph (5) provides that the sheriff is to consider "the circumstances of the parties and whether (and to what extent) they are represented". This acknowledges

---

[34] r.9.3(2).

[35] 1990 S.C.L.R. 369.

[36] This will avoid the situation which arose in *Dunn v Hall* where a solicitor claimed that he had been so surprised by the course that the hearing took that he failed to request an opportunity to lead evidence.

that, apart from both parties being professionally represented or both representing themselves, there are other possibilities. For example, only one side may be professionally represented, or one or both sides may turn up with what rule 2.1 terms an "authorised lay representative". Authorised lay representatives take different forms. Some are quite experienced in representing clients in various fora while others may have little experience. Some will barely merit the name "representative", having come along to lend moral support to a very apprehensive friend or relative.

The appropriate way to deal with these situations will vary. Sub-paragraph (5)(a) and (b) indicate the action that sheriffs should consider in the light of the circumstances with which they are faced. They may put questions to parties and to witnesses and, if they think that it is necessary to the fair conduct of the hearing, explain any legal terms or expressions which are used. Sub-paragraph (6) provides that evidence will normally be taken on oath or affirmation but gives sheriffs discretion to dispense with that requirement where they think it reasonable to do so.

The discussion of the Hearing noted that rules 9.4 and 9.5 permit sheriffs to inspect places and objects and remit a matter of fact to an appropriate person. The facilities can also be invoked at the hearing with evidence. It would seem unlikely that a remit would be made at this stage as that is a decision that ought to have been made at the Hearing which should have identified the importance of the factual issue requiring a report. It is, however, quite possible that an inspection might be thought appropriate at this stage.

Rule 9.2(4) envisages that parties will have to lead evidence on disputed issues of fact. Like rule 16 in the original rules, there is no reference to a right to cross examine. In the context of the informal conduct of small claims hearings this is important and serves to prevent the problem that has arisen in England arising in Scotland.

Specifically to assist those bringing small claims, s.35 of the Sheriff Courts Scotland Act 1971 provides that "no enactment or rule of law or relating to admissibility of corroboration of evidence before a court of law shall be binding in a small claim." In so far as its provisions are more extensive, reference to the Civil Evidence (Scotland) Act 1988 may also be of assistance. Section 1 of the Act abolishes the rule requiring corroboration, and s.2 deals with the admissibility of hearsay evidence. No longer is evidence excluded solely because it is hearsay, and a court or jury, if satisfied that the fact has been established by evidence, shall be entitled to find that fact proved notwithstanding that the evidence is hearsay. A statement made by a person otherwise than in the course of the proof is admissible as evidence of any matter contained in the statement of which direct oral evidence by that person would be admissible.

It is the responsibility of the parties to secure the attendance of their own witnesses and they are personally liable for their expenses.[37] Where citation of witnesses is necessary they must be given at least seven days notice of the hearing at which they are to appear.[38] The summons or the copy served on the defender is sufficient warrant for the citation of witnesses. If a witness, having been properly cited and offered travelling expenses, where they have been requested, fails to answer the citation the sheriff may impose on him a penalty not exceeding £250 unless he offers a reasonable excuse.[39] The sheriff may grant decree for payment of this penalty to the party on whose behalf the witness was cited.[40] The sheriff also has power under rule 17.6(4) to grant a warrant to compel the attendance of witness. Such a warrant may be executed in any sheriffdom without endorsation, and the expenses of it may be awarded against the witness. Small claim rule 17.6(1) provides that the hearing of a small claim shall not be adjourned solely on account of the failure of a witness to appear unless the sheriff on cause shown so directs.

Productions

Unless the sheriff permits or the parties agree, a party may only found at a hearing on documents or articles in the three circumstances set out in rule 16.1(3). First, where the documents or articles are in the possession of the party and are reasonably capable of being lodged with the court they must be lodged with the sheriff clerk 14 days before the hearing.[41] A list of the items must be given to the sheriff clerk and also sent to the other party. Secondly, documents or articles produced at an earlier hearing may be relied on, and, finally, documents recovered by the procedure set out in rule 18.

A party litigant is not permitted to borrow productions unless he has the leave of the sheriff but may inspect them during normal office hours at the sheriff clerk's office and, where practicable, obtain copies.[42] Where productions are borrowed, as they may be by solicitors, or by others if so permitted, receipts for them shall be entered in the inventory of productions and they shall be returned not later than noon on the day

---

[37] r.17.4.
[38] r.17.4(4).
[39] r.17.6(2).
[40] r.17.6(3).
[41] r.16.1(1)(a).
[42] r.16.2(4) and (5).

before the full hearing.[43] Documents or other productions referred to
during a hearing, and a report of a person to whom a matter has been
remitted, shall be retained in the custody of the sheriff clerk until any
appeal has been disposed of.[44]

Judgment

The sheriff makes notes of the evidence at the hearing for his own use
and retains these notes until after any appeal has been disposed of.[45]
Rule 9.8 provides that the sheriff should, where practicable, give his
decision and a brief statement of his reasons at the conclusion of the
hearing. If he reserves judgment he or she must, within 28 days, produce
a written decision with a brief note of reasons which the sheriff clerk
intimates to the parties.[46]

Having pronounced judgment, the sheriff then deals with expenses
and proceeds to grant a decree as appropriate. In a small claim this is a
final decree.[47] Prior to granting decree the defender, where it is competent to do so, may apply for a time to pay direction. This he may do
orally or in writing.[48]

OTHER HEARINGS

In addition to the two main types of hearing, the Hearing and the hearing
on evidence, four other types are possible. The purpose and conduct of
an appeal are discussed in Chapter 6. The three other types of hearing
are: those on a time to pay application or time order in an undefended
claim where the pursuer has not accepted the defender's written proposals or the defender wishes to make a proposal in court; a hearing on
a minute for recall of a decree; and a hearing of an incidental application. These are subject to the provisions about the conduct of hearings
in general and reference should be made to the comments above.
Indeed, the first and third of these will often take place during the
Hearing.

---

[43] r.16.2(2).
[44] r.16.4(2).
[45] r.9.6.
[46] r.9.8(2).
[47] r.9.8(3) and (4).
[48] r.9.7.

Representation

In another acknowledgment of the practical problems of embarking on litigation, the normal rules about representation have been relaxed. In addition to representing him or herself a party may be represented by an advocate, solicitor or an authorised lay representative.[49] An authorised lay representative may in representing a party "do everything for the preparation and conduct of a small claim as may be done by an individual conducting his own claim".[50] Authorised lay representatives must be able to demonstrate that they are in fact the approved representatives of the parties for whom they purport to act. This will not present a problem where the party is present in court. Where this is not so it would be sensible for the representative to have written authorisation.

If the representative does not have the authorisation of the party he or she must cease to act as a representative. The sheriff may also require an authorised lay representative to cease to represent a party where it is found that the representative is "not a suitable person to represent the party".[51] In practice, this has permitted employees to act as representatives as well as relatives, friends and staff or volunteers from advice agencies such as the Citizens' Advice Bureaux, or trading standards staff.

Rule 1.1(2) contains an important reference to "authorised lay representative". It states that this means "a person to whom section 32(1) of the Solicitors (Scotland) Act 1980 . . . does not apply by virtue of section 32(2)(a) of that Act". This leads into one of the unhappier pieces of drafting in relation to small claims. The purpose is partly to overcome a problem that was identified in the *Dana* case in relation to employees who were not legally qualified drafting small claim documents. Under the original version of s.32 of the Solicitors (Scotland) Act 1980 such people might be said to have infringed the ban on unqualified persons drafting "any writ relating to any action or proceedings in any court". There was (and still is) an exemption for those who do this without fee or reward or the expectation of such fee or reward. That would have protected lay representatives such as the Citizens' Advice Bureaux volunteers or a relative who helped a party without any thought of remuneration. It was thought that paid employees of the litigant could not take advantage of the exemption.

The current version of s.32 still makes it a criminal offence for unqualified people to, amongst other things, draft "any writ relating to

---

[49] r.2.1(1).
[50] r.2.1(2).
[51] r.2.1(3).

any action or proceedings in any court".[52] Paid employees are doubly protected in relation to small claims by the current amended version of s.32. Because they are authorised lay representatives for the purposes of small claim procedure that offence is not committed by them because of s.32(2B). That subsection states:

> "Subsection (1)(b) shall not apply to a person who is, by virtue of any act of sederunt made under section 32 (power of Court of Session to regulate procedure) of the Sheriff Courts (Scotland) Act 1971, permitted to represent a party to a summary cause."

The Small Claim Rules 2002 is such an act of sederunt; and authorised lay representatives are persons "permitted to represent a party to a summary cause".

Paid employees can be said to be doubly protected because in addition to protection just outlined there is further protection in s.32(2)(a). This provides that an unqualified person who drafts documents relating to legal proceedings does not commit an offence:

> "if he proves that he drew or prepared the writ or papers in question without receiving, or without expecting to receive, either directly or indirectly, any fee, gain or reward (*other than remuneration paid under a contract of employment*)." [emphasis added]

This is not unnecessary duplication. Section 32(2B) applies only to summary cause procedure of which small claim is a species whereas s.32(2)(a) applies to all forms of procedure. Employees need this protection if their companies wish, for example, to litigate under ordinary cause procedure without engaging a solicitor.

What of the position of authorised lay representatives other than employees? The import of the legislation discussed above is not simply that they are entitled to draft documents and represent people in small claim procedure but that this could be done for reward. This is the clear effect of s.32(2B). For the purposes of small claim procedure the ban on preparing documents relating to litigation contained in s.32(1)(b) does not apply to any unqualified person. That is as far as it goes. The prohibition applies to all other forms of procedure subject, of course, to the qualification contained in s.32(2)(a) in relation to acting gratuitously. The conclusion is that the way is open for a new breed of unqualified litigator in the sheriff courts. In practice such a development seems unlikely as the economics of such an adventure are not likely to be attractive.

---

[52] s.32(1)(b).

CHAPTER 6

APPEALS, EXPENSES AND MISCELLANEOUS MATTERS

In the interests of speedy and inexpensive settlement of cases it is usual in small claim procedures to withdraw or restrict the right of appeal. In this procedure an appeal to the Sheriff Principal on a point of law from the final judgment of the sheriff is permitted. Unlike conventional summary cause no further appeal is permitted[1] except in the case of time to pay orders where the right to appeal is governed by s.103 of the Debtors (Scotland) Act 1987. There does not appear to be any method of appealing against the interim interlocutor of the sheriff. In summary cause it has been held that there is no appeal at common law even though the sheriff may have pronounced an incompetent interlocutor.[2] In a procedure intended to be informal and quick this is hardly surprising.

There has been some litigation about what amounts to a "final judgment". In *Webster Engineering Services Ltd v Gibson*[3] Sheriff Principal Caplan gave guidance on the correct approach. He said:

"The words 'from the final judgment of the sheriff' may suggest that the point of law requires to be one fundamental to the fabric of the sheriff's decision. However, I think that view may be unduly restrictive and that the application of the relevant stipulation can be applied to all points of law bearing upon the final judgment . . . The effect of [s.38], in my view is to allow an appeal to the Sheriff Principal against any final judgment, provided that it is on a point of law. However, other appeals, that is to say appeals on questions of fact or on interlocutors which are not final judgments, are expressly disallowed."

In that case a claim had been dismissed as provided by the summary cause rules when neither party had appeared at the proof. The pursuers appealed to the Sheriff Principal and requested him to exercise the

[1] Sheriff Courts (Scotland) Act 1971, s.38.
[2] *L Mackinnon & Son v Coles*, Sheriff Bell, Aberdeen Sh.Ct, January 13, 1984, unreported; cited in MacPhail (2nd ed.), Vol.1, para.18.12.
[3] 1987 S.L.T. (Sh.Ct.) 101.

dispensing power. The appeal was allowed. In *Rediffusion v McIlroy*[4] the appeal was against the refusal of the sheriff to adjourn a proof which had the result that a decree by consent was granted. The appeal was refused because it was an appeal against an interlocutory judgment. In *W Jack Baillie Associates v Kennedy*[5] an appeal against the refusal of a sheriff to exercise the dispensing power to receive late a minute recalling a decree was regarded as incompetent even though the refusal, in a sense, decided the outcome of the action. Sheriff Principal Caplan observed that "refusal to allow an extension of time is truly procedural in character and in no way can be said to have a direct effect on the issues of the case".

The procedure for appeals is set out in Chapter 23 of the rules, which deals differently with appeals against time to pay directions and other appeals. In the case of an appeal other than one against a time to pay direction the method is by note of appeal in Form 21. This must be lodged with the sheriff clerk not later than 14 days after the date of the final decree. The note must request a stated case and specify the point of law on which the appeal is based.[6] At the same time as lodging the note of appeal the appellant must intimate a copy to every other party to the claim.[7] Within a further 28 days the sheriff must issue a draft stated case containing findings in fact and law or, where appropriate, a narrative of the proceedings before him, appropriate questions of law, and a note stating the reasons for his decisions in law.[8] This is sent to the parties who have 14 days to lodge a note of any adjustments with the sheriff clerk, and the respondent may state any point of law which he wishes to raise on appeal. Such adjustments or points of law are intimated to the other party.[9] Fourteen days after the latest date on which a note of adjustments has been or may be lodged, or the date of a hearing on adjustments, the sheriff states and signs the stated case.[10] The hearing on adjustments may be permitted of the sheriff's own motion or on the motion of a party.[11] Where the sheriff proposes to reject an adjustment a hearing must be held.[12]

In *Mannifield v Douglas Walker*[13] Sheriff Principal Nicholson made some observations on the form of the stated case. The stated case, as

---

[4] 1986 S.L.T. (Sh.Ct.) 33.
[5] 1985 S.L.T. (Sh.Ct.) 53.
[6] r.23.1(1).
[7] r.23.1(2).
[8] r.23.1(3).
[9] r.23.1(4).
[10] r.23.1(8).
[11] r.23.1(5).
[12] r.23.1(5).
[13] 1990 S.C.L.R. 369.

was permissible under original rule 29(3)(a) which is replaced in the new rules, contained no express findings of fact and law but instead contained a narrative of what emerged during the hearing, followed by a note. The Sheriff Principal observed:

> "I have had difficulty in this case in determining exactly what facts the sheriff found to be proved and I suspect that there might have been no such difficulty had the sheriff followed the familiar prac- tice of setting out specific findings. Given the alternative practice permitted by the rule referred to above, I do not go so far as to say that a sheriff should always state express findings in fact in a stated case. I consider, however, that it will be helpful if, by some means or another, a sheriff makes absolutely clear in a stated case what facts he found to be established."

After a notice of appeal has been lodged in a small claim the appellant may not withdraw it without the consent of the other parties, or by leave of the Sheriff Principal, and on such terms as to expenses or otherwise as seem proper to him.[14]

The sheriff may regulate all matters relating to interim possession, make any order for preservation of property to which the action relates, or for its sale, if perishable, or for the preservation of evidence. He or she may make in his or her discretion any interim order which a due regard for the interests of the parties may require.[15] The stated case shall include questions of law framed by the sheriff arising from the points of law stated by the parties and such other questions of law as he may consider appropriate.[16] The sheriff clerk then places before the Sheriff Principal all documents and productions in the claim together with the stated case and sends to the parties a copy of the stated case together with a note of the date, time and place of the hearing of the appeal.[17] At the hearing of the appeal a party shall not be allowed to raise questions of law of which notice has not been given except on cause shown and subject to such conditions as to expenses or otherwise as the Sheriff Principal may consider appropriate.[18]

In addition, a point of law may not be appealable because it was not noted as a disputed issue at the Hearing. This point arose in *Kostric v J. O'Hara Car Sales*[19] where the dispute concerned a defective second-

---

[14] r.23.2.
[15] r.23.5.
[16] r.23.1(8).
[17] r.23.1(9).
[18] r.23.2.
[19] 1990 S.C.L.R. 129.

hand car. At the preliminary hearing, despite the fact that a fairly lengthy written defence had been lodged, the only disputed issue noted by the sheriff was: "It was not Mr. O'Hara but someone else", meaning that he was not responsible for the turning back of the odometer. In these circumstances the Sheriff Principal doubted the propriety of permitting one of the questions in law in the stated case which was "Did I properly interpret the Sale of Goods Act 1979 in determining whether the basis for the pursuers case was established both generally and in respect of damages?" The Sheriff Principal pointed out that, as the question had not been noted as a disputed issue at the preliminary hearing, it was unnecessary for the pursuer to satisfy the sheriff that the facts relied on and established by him were sufficient in law to found his claim, and it was not open to the defender to raise this issue on appeal. On the other hand, questions of how far the sheriff's decision was justified in law by the evidence could not have been put in issue before the hearing and thus could be raised on appeal.

In addition to the question of whether the evidence supported the decision the stated case also asked: "Had I exercised to my discretion in such a manner as to arrive at a decision that no Sheriff properly directing himself in law could properly have arrived at?" This the Sheriff Principal refused "with some hesitation" to answer because "insofar as it covers any different ground from [the question whether the evidence supported the decision] . . . , it seems to me that it opens the way to an appeal on the question of whether the sheriff was right in his assessment of the evidence, which is, to my mind, an appeal on fact and not a question of law."

It is suggested that this was the correct approach provided that it is not taken too literally. While one might expect precise reference to statutory provisions where a party is represented it should be considered acceptable, when this is not the case, if it is clear that the issue of whether the appropriate legal test was met, was raised. The necessity for the Hearing to be conducted with care again becomes apparent.

Where the appeal is solely in relation to a time to pay direction rule 23.4 applies a different procedure. The rules relating to the formulation of other appeals are disapplied. This type of appeal requires leave to appeal from the sheriff who made the decision. This is sought within seven days of the decision by applying on Form 22, stating the question of law on which the appeal is to proceed.[20] If leave to appeal is granted, the appeal must be lodged in Form 23 and intimated by the appellant to

---

[20] r.23.4(3).

every other party within 14 days of the order granting leave and the sheriff must state in writing his reasons for the original decision.[21]

An appeal to the Sheriff Principal proceeds in accordance with paragraphs (1), (4) and (5) of rule 23.3 which provide that the Sheriff Principal shall hear the parties or their solicitors orally on all matters connected with the appeal, including liability for expenses. If any party moves that the question of liability for expenses be heard after the Sheriff Principal has given his decision the sheriff may grant the motion. The Sheriff Principal may adhere to or vary the decree appealed against or recall the decree and substitute another therefor, or remit, if he considers it desirable, to the sheriff, for any reason other than having further evidence led. At the conclusion of the hearing the Sheriff Principal may pronounce his decision or reserve judgment. In the latter case he shall within 28 days give his decision in writing and the sheriff clerk shall forthwith intimate it to the parties.

Conduct of appeal hearing

Rule 9.2 dealing with the conduct of hearings applies to appeals. In practice in the vast majority of appeals both sides have been represented by solicitors and they have been conducted like any other appeal in the sheriff court. Where one or both parties is not represented it will be necessary to taken into account the guidance given in the rule.

EXPENSES

The usual practice is that expenses follow success. That principle is widely believed to be a major deterrent to the use of the courts, particularly where relatively small amounts are at stake. It was, therefore, essential that the normal rule be modified if the small claims procedure was to be attractive to potential litigants. This was all the more necessary since the legal aid scheme does not extend to small claims.[22] The Legal Advice and Assistance scheme can, of course be used, to advise a potential litigant.

Section 36B of the Sheriff Courts (Scotland) Act 1971 provides that, where the value of a claim does not exceed an amount to be determined by the Lord Advocate, no award of expenses will be made; and in other

---

[21] r.23.4(4).
[22] Legal Aid (Scotland) Act 1986, Sch.2, Pt II, para.3.

small claims expenses will be limited to an amount determined by the Lord Advocate. The Small Claims (Scotland) Order 1998 set these amounts were set at £200 and £75 respectively.

These modifications of the normal rule do not apply in certain circumstances set out in s.36B(3) of the Sheriff Courts (Scotland) Act 1971 (the effect of which is reproduced in small claims rule 26). Section 36B(3) states:

> "Subsections (1) and (2) above do not apply to a party to a small claim—
>   (a) who being a defender—
>   (i) has not stated a defence
>   (ii) having stated a defence, has not proceeded with it; or
>   (iii) having stated and proceeded with a defence, has not acted in good faith as to its merits; or
>   (b) on whose part there has been unreasonable conduct in relation to the proceedings or the claim; nor do they apply in relation to an appeal to the sheriff principal."

There are five situations in which the protection against paying expenses on the normal basis is removed. Where an appeal is made to the Sheriff Principal expenses are awarded on the normal basis.[23] Of the other four the first three of apply to defenders and the fourth to all parties. The protection is lost where no defence has been stated. This is very common as the vast majority of small claim actions are debt collection actions which are not defended. In addition to the claim where there is no response from the defender there are cases where the response will not be treated as amounting to a proper defence. A good example is *Hamilton v Ansah*,[24] discussed in Chapter 5.

It should be noted that Rule 9.1, the first in the group of rules under the heading "Defended claim", distinguishes between stating a defence and disputing the amount of the claim. The defender's copy summons Forms 1a and 1b reflect this in section B, the "Defender's Response to the Summons" which in Box 3 offers amongst the possible responses: "I wish to dispute the amount due only; and I intend to state a defence". Both these responses are ways of stating a defence and entitle the defender to the protection of the rules limiting expenses. In one case there is a defence on the merits and on the other a defence on quantum. The rule may well have been drafted in this way to make it clear to lay

---

[23] Sheriff Court (Scotland) Act 1971, s.36B(3) and r.21.6(1)(b).
[24] 1990 S.C.L.R. 21.

defenders, who may not seek professional help, that not only may they resist the claim by denying liability but also by admitting liability and disputing the amount for which they re liable.

Having stated a defence has not proceeded with it

To obtain protection from the full rigour of the rules on expenses it is necessary not only to state a defence but to proceed with it. This has provoked a number of appeals in cases where a defence was stated but before a full hearing was held the defender had conceded the claim. Such cases, as Sheriff Principal MacLeod pointed out in *Gilmour v Patterson*,[25] could not strictly speaking be said to have been settled as there was no agreement on expenses. The defenders claimed to be entitled to the protection of the small claim expenses rules. It was held in *Gilmour v Patterson* that the effect of rule 26 of the original rules (which is in similar terms to rule 21.6) was that only a defender who stated a defence and in good faith proceeded with it was protected from an award of expenses on the summary cause scale. To the argument that this approach would encourage defenders to persist with defences rather than settling the Sheriff Principal pointed out that:

> "Any defender who proceeds through to proof after, at some stage, coming to the conclusion that his defence is without merit, is at least at risk of being identified by the court as having not acted in good faith, in which event the summary cause scale of expenses would be held to apply. The rule is expressed in terms which invite a court to consider whether an unsuccessful defender has acted in good faith as to the merits of his defence."[26]

In *Glover v Deighan*, 1992 S.L.T. (Sh.Ct.) 88 Sheriff Principal Hay followed *Gilmour v Patterson*. He saw no distinction between the circumstances of a payment action in that case and a personal injury action such as the case before him. He summed up the correct approach as follows:

> "If the defender does not defend the claim and decree passes against him in absence, expenses will be awarded on the summary cause scale. Similarly, in my opinion, expenses on the summary cause scale fall to be awarded where a defence is stated initially but

---

[25] 1992 S.L.T. (Sh.Ct.) 10.
[26] *ibid.* at 12.

the claim is subsequently met, whether in full or by compromised settlement. The only exception will be in a case where the parties agree otherwise in relation to expenses."

Having stated a defence has not proceeded with it in good faith

As was pointed out in *Gilmour v Patterson*, the protection from expenses on the normal summary cause scale will also be lost where the defence has not been proceeded with in good faith. In that case it was suggested that to persevere with a defence after coming to the conclusion that it was without merit would amount to proceeding in bad faith.

Either party's unreasonable conduct in relation to the proceedings or the claim

In addition to the circumstances where a defender may lose the protection of the expenses rules which are contained in s.36B(3)(a), subs.(3)(b) provides that any party "on whose part there has been unreasonable conduct in relation to the proceedings or the claim" will also do so. This provision was discussed by Sheriff Principal Nicholson in *Milne v Uniroyal Englebert Tyres Ltd.*[27] In that case, following a full hearing, the sheriff had found in favour of the defenders because he preferred their evidence to that of the pursuer. The defenders sought unrestricted expenses on the ground that the case put forward in the summons was not substantiated by his evidence.

The Sheriff Principal first noted that it would be a mistake to treat the subsection as dealing with something other than lack of good faith because subsection 3(a) refers to absence of good faith on the part of a defender. He observed:

"that subs (3) (b) could embrace an absence of good faith on the part of a defender in circumstances that would not be struck at by the earlier provision, and I certainly consider that the subsection is apt to include cases where there is an absence of good faith on the part of a pursuer. But, the general nature of the term 'unreasonable conduct' must, I think, include more than just an absence of good faith since otherwise there would have been no reason for the subsection to use that term rather than simply repeating the express

[27] 1995 S.L.T. (Sh.Ct.) 23.

reference to an absence of good faith which is to be found in the preceding subsection."

After commenting that it would not be prudent or possible to give an exhaustive definition of lack of good faith because the circumstances in which the issue could arise were so various the Sheriff Principal said:

"I have come to the conclusion that in a case like the present one, where a pursuer's evidence at proof does not match the case which he has put forward initially, it will be necessary to come close to the position of being able to say that he has knowingly put forward a false case before it can be said that he has been guilty of unreasonable conduct in relation to either the proceedings or the claim. As was said by the solicitor for the pursuer, it is by no means uncommon for a pursuer to fail in an action because, at the end of the day, his evidence does not measure up to what has been stated in the pleadings; and in my opinion it would be difficult, if not impossible, to say that that alone was sufficient to justify a finding of unreasonable conduct."

An important factor in coming to this conclusion was that the pursuer had been represented by competent and experienced solicitors throughout the proceedings. The Sheriff Principal considered that to have exposed him to payment of expenses on the summary cause scale would have been unfair in the circumstances. He thought that, where a party had followed the advice of his solicitors, he should not lose the protection of the expenses rules unless he had "in effect deceived both his own solicitors and others by knowingly putting forward a false claim".

In *Penman v North British Steel Group*[28] the pursuer's action in seeking expenses where the quantum had been agreed extra-judicially but agreement could not be obtained on expenses was not unreasonable. Further guidance may be found in the existing case law on expenses in other procedures. Failure to give the defender any warning of an intention to raise an action would probably amount to unreasonable conduct as was held in *Cellular Clothing Co Ltd v Sculberg*.[29] In some circumstances where, as in *Gunn v Hunter*,[30] a tender was not accepted originally but accepted after the action was raised, the conduct of the pursuer might be regarded as unreasonable. Failure to attend a hearing,

---

[28] 1991 S.L.T. (Sh.Ct.) 45.
[29] 1952 S.L.T. (Notes) 73. In *Taylor v Borthwick*, 1990 S.C.L.R. 44 the argument that the claim had been raised prematurely without the courtesy of a warning letter failed on the facts.
[30] (1886) 13 R. 573.

while not completely depriving the guilty party of the protection of the expenses rules might well be a ground for some departure from them.[31]

Litigant in person

Prior to the Litigants in Person (Costs and Expenses) Act 1975 a party litigant, *i.e.* someone other than a practising solicitor who conducts his own cause, was not entitled to charge for time and trouble expended on the case. There was also some doubt as to the extent to which such litigants could recover outlays. The 1975 Act and the Act of Sederunt (Expenses of Party Litigants) 1976,[32] as amended by the Act of Sederunt (Expenses of Party Litigants) 1983,[33] now permit this. The party litigant may recover such sums as appear to the auditor to be reasonable having regard to all the circumstances in respect of work done which was reasonably required in connection with the cause, up to a maximum of two-thirds of the sum allowable to a solicitor; and outlays reasonably incurred for the proper conduct of the cause. In assessing these expenses the auditor may take into consideration the nature of the work, the time taken and the time reasonably required to do the work, the amount of time spent in respect of which there was no loss of earnings, lost earnings, and the complexity of the litigation and its importance to the litigant. As a result of the 1983 amendments to the Act of Sederunt which removed the distinction between remunerative time and leisure time, expenses awardable to a party litigant should now be somewhat more generous.

It would appear that as the term party litigant has been judicially defined as anyone other than a practising solicitor who conducts a cause, representatives permitted under rule 30 will be able to obtain expenses[34] under the 1975 Act.

A solicitor who conducts his own case and is awarded expenses is entitled to make professional charges for those parts of the case where a solicitor would have been required if the party had not been a solicitor.[35] Where an appeal is taken the special rules about expenses do

---

[31] This would be consistent with the power in the Act of Sederunt (Fees of Solicitors in the Sheriff Court) 1989 (SI 1989 No. 434) which gives the sheriff discretion to modify expenses where one party fails to turn up or is not in a position to go ahead.

[32] SI 1976/1606.

[33] SI 1983/143.

[34] *Macbeth, Currie and Co v Matthew*, 1985 S.L.T. (Sh.Ct.) 44.

[35] *ibid.*

not apply and in relation to the appeal expenses are assessed on the summary cause scale.[36]

Problems areas

Problems can arise because of the restrictions on expenses and the absence of legal aid; and also where the value of the claim is in the region of the upper limit of small claims. These problems have tended to arise in relation to personal injury claims though they need not be confined to them. It has already been seen that in straightforward personal injury claims attempts to avoid the expenses rule of small claims procedure by raising an action as a conventional summary cause have not always found favour with sheriffs.[37] However, in *Whyte v D.B. Marshall Ltd.*[38] Sheriff Wheatley took a different view. In that case and a parallel case the pursuers had raised summary cause actions for £1,000 in respect of personal injuries. Both cases were settled extra-judicially by means of a tender and acceptance for, in one case £575, and in the other £380. The question at the hearing was what measure of expenses was appropriate. The pursuer argued that the value of the claim must be taken as the value of the settlement and the fact that an action was raised as a summary cause did not necessarily mean that the pursuer would invariably be entitled to expenses on the summary cause scale. It was pointed out that the action could have been raised as a small claim and, if appropriate, applied to have it remitted to the summary cause roll. The sheriff preferred the submissions of the agent for the pursuers that in a claim of this sort to restrict the pursuer to small claims expenses would cause substantial prejudice and could in effect preclude a pursuer from raising and action because the limit of such expenses would not on any view cover the necessary costs involved in raising an action. He added:

> "I think it would be intolerable, and something which was certainly not within the contemplation of parliament when these rules were made, that the pursuer should have to pay a substantial proportion of the expenses necessary to raise an action out of any damages he or she might subsequently obtain. I am satisfied that such would be the position here. Further, I do not think that the defender's position is necessarily prejudiced because the pursuer chooses to take

---

[36] Sheriff Court (Scotland) Act 1971, s.36B(3).
[37] *Robertson v DB Marshall (Newbridge) Ltd*, 1989 S.L.T. (Sh.Ct.) 102; *Gorham v GB Papers Ltd*, Cupar Sheriff Court.
[38] Perth Sheriff Court, September 25, 1989, unreported.

a summary cause action rather than by means of the small claim procedure. The defender's position in these circumstances can always be safeguarded by the opportunity, taken in the present case, to argue that in the circumstances expenses should be restricted to the small claims level."

It may be that there is no conflict between this decision and that of Sheriff Macphail in *Robertson v D.B. Marshall (Newbridge) Ltd.* as there is some suggestion in Sheriff Principal Wheatley's judgement that the case involved the interpretation of a provision of the Factories Acts. For another approach to the problem the judgment of Sheriff McInnes in *Graham v Murray*[39] is of interest. The pursuer raised a summary cause action for personal injuries claiming £1,500 after negotiations on quantum had broken down. The defender tendered £750 which was accepted on the basis that expenses would be decided by the court as the defender was not prepared to offer more than would be payable for a case settling within the small claims limit. The sheriff ordered that expenses on the summary cause scale should be awarded because it was reasonable to have raised the action as a summary cause. He pointed out that the difficulties of valuing personal injuries cases were well known and that it was correct for the pursuer's solicitor to have valued the claim in excess of £750. That there was correspondence indicating that the pursuer might at one time have settled for less than £750 and did settle for that sum did not affect this conclusion. The sheriff acknowledged that people settle claims for less than a court might award for all sorts of reasons. As he pointed out this case was distinguishable from *Robertson v D.B. Marshall (Newbridge) Ltd.* in that in *Robertson* there was never any suggestion that the claim was worth more than £750.

Procedure
Expenses are usually dealt with immediately after the sheriff has pronounced his decision as provided by rule 21.6(6). That rule provides that this will not be the case where judgment has been reserved or the sheriff orders otherwise as might be the case where there is some complication in deciding on the amount of expenses. The successful party makes a motion for expenses. It was held in *Stewart Saunders Ltd v Arun Gupta*[40] that a further motion that expenses be awarded on the normal basis rather than under the rules restricting small claim expenses does

[39] Cupar Sheriff Court, April 19, 1990, unreported.
[40] 1992 S.C.L.R. 802.

not need to be made by incidental application and thus require notice. However, the sheriff did observe in that case that the circumstances of the application might justify holding a separate hearing on expenses.

Rule 21.6(5) provides that in every case, including an appeal, where expenses are awarded, the sheriff clerk shall hear the parties or their solicitors on the claims for expenses. It is the duty of the sheriff clerk, with the approval of the sheriff, to assess the amount of expenses in accordance with the statutory table of fees of solicitors appropriate to summary cause.[41] Where the rules limiting the level of expenses apply this task is not likely to be onerous as the upper limit on expenses of £75 will easily be met by professional charges. Even in the case where the successful party is a party litigant it will be fairly easy to reach the limit when one takes account of the fee on the summons which is currently £39. In *Sloan v Mycock*[42] it was held that where there were several defenders against whom a claim failed the aggregate total of expenses payable by the pursuer was £75.

Where the hearing on expenses is not heard immediately after the sheriff has given his decision the sheriff clerk fixes a date, time and place for a hearing giving all parties at least 14 days notice in writing.[43] The party awarded expenses must lodge an account of expenses in court at least seven days before the date of the hearing and at the same time forward a copy of that account to the other parties.[44] At the hearing the sheriff clerk decides on the amount of expenses and reports the decision to the Sheriff Principal (in the case of an appeal) or the sheriff in open court for his approval. Notice of this hearing will have been given to the parties by the sheriff clerk.[45] At the hearing the Sheriff Principal or sheriff hears any objections of the parties and then pronounces final decree in the claim including decree for payment of expenses.[46]

Should any party fail to comply with the provisions of rule 21.6 or the successful party fail to appear at the hearing on expenses this fact must be reported to the sheriff at a diet which has been intimated to the parties.[47] Unless sufficient cause is shown, the sheriff must pronounce decree on the merits of the claim and find no expenses due to or by any party.[48]

---

[41] r.21.6(2).
[42] 1992 S.L.T. (Sh.Ct.) 23.
[43] r.21.6(7).
[44] r.21.6(8).
[45] r.21.6(9).
[46] r.21.6(10).
[47] r.21.6(12).
[48] r.21.6(13).

The Sheriff Principal or sheriff may, if he thinks fit, on the application of the solicitor of any party to whom expenses may be awarded, grant decree to that solicitor for the expenses of the claim.[49]

DECREE AND ENFORCEMENT

A decree of the sheriff in a small claim shall be a final decree.[50] Whether the decree is against the defender in respect of a claim or a pursuer in relation to a counterclaim the sheriff must be satisfied that there is a ground of jurisdiction.[51] At any time before extract, that is, before the document of the sheriff clerk certifying that the decree has been made is issued, the sheriff may correct any clerical or incidental error in the interlocutor or note attached to it.[52] As with conventional summary cause, a decree in a small claim may be issued only after the lapse of 14 days from the granting of the decree. There is power in rule 21.5(1) for the sheriff to grant an extract decree earlier. This requires the party of requesting the earlier issuing of the decree to make an incidental application.[53] If an appeal has been lodged the extract must not be issued until the appeal has been disposed of.[54] The extract decree may be written on the summons or a separate paper. Forms 18 to 18i set out the various types of decree that can be issued.[55] When issued the extract decree is warrant for "all lawful diligence proceeding thereon."[56] In the case of actions for delivery rule 21.9 applies and the pursuer may apply to the court to grant a warrant to search for and take possession of the goods of which delivery is sought. The warrant applies only to premises occupied by the defender and may be executed only after the expiry of a charge following upon decree of delivery.

In *Bruckash Ltd v Lonie*[57] it was decided that while the holder of a decree may take steps in another sheriff court district or sheriffdom once goods are poinded, warrant to sell must be obtained from the court from which the decree emanated.

---

[49] r.21.6(15).
[50] r.29(4).
[51] r.21.1.
[52] r.21.4.
[53] r.21.5(2).
[54] r.21.5(3).
[55] r.21.5(4).
[56] r.21.5(4)(c).
[57] 1990 S.C.L.R. 529.

REMITS

The circumstances in which, under s.37 of the Sheriff Courts (Scotland) Act 1971, remits may be made to or from small claims have been discussed above.[58] Rule 15.2 deals with remits between procedures. Where a direction has been made by the sheriff under s.37(2B) of the Sheriff Courts (Scotland) Act 1971 that a small claim be treated as a summary cause he or she must specify the next step of procedure to be followed. Where the small claim is being transferred to the ordinary cause rule 15.2(1) sets out in more detail the directions to be given by the sheriff. The pursuer will be directed to lodge an initial writ and intimate to it to every other party within 14 days of the date of the direction. The defender will be directed to lodge defences within 28 days of the date of the direction. Finally, a date and time for an options hearing must be fixed. This must be more than 10 weeks after the last date for lodging the initial writ, though the sheriff may choose "such lesser period as he considers appropriate".

Where the transfer is in the opposite direction and an ordinary cause or summary cause is to be treated as a small claim it calls at the Hearing referred to in rule 9.1.

TRANSFER

Rule 15.1 provides that "The sheriff may transfer a claim to any other sheriff court, whether in the same sheriffdom or not, if the sheriff considers that it is expedient to do so." In addition, the same rule provides that where the sheriff finds that his court has no jurisdiction he may transfer the claim to the one where it ought to have been brought. In these cases "A claim so transferred shall proceed in all respects as if it had been brought originally in the court to which it is transferred."

This gives the sheriff a very wide discretion and it appears that, while a transfer will normally be made on the motion of one of the parties, it is permissible for the sheriff to act of his own motion.[59]

[58] See pp.12–14.
[59] *Macphail* (2nd ed.), Vol.1, para.13–50.

RECALL OF A DECREE

In certain circumstances an application may be made to recall a decree though this may only be done on one occasion. Recall is possible where a decree has been granted:

(a) under rule 8.1(3) to a pursuer where no response to the summons has been received from the defender;

(b) to a pursuer where the defender has not appeared or been represented at the Hearing and the pursuer has appeared[60];

(c) to a defender where the pursuer has not appeared or been represented at the Hearing and the defender has appeared[61];

(d) neither party appears at the Hearing[62];

(e) to a defender where a counterclaim has been stated in the absence of the pursuer. In these circumstances the hearing will have been continued to allow the pursuer to respond to the counterclaim and if he or she fails to appear or be represented at the continuation decree in absence will be granted.[63]

What constitutes an application?
There has been some controversy in relation to the procedure to be adopted when a party who has lodged a minute for recall of the decree fails to appear at the hearing arranged. As the current rule is in the same terms as the original rule there is case law of assistance. In *Alpine House Ltd v Links*[64] Sheriff Principal Hay followed Sheriff Principal MacLeod's decision in *Sureweld (UK) Ltd v DS Baddeley (Engineers) Ltd*[65] and held that the correct practice was for a minute of recall to be dropped from the roll if no-one appeared to move it. In *Reid Furniture Company Ltd v Coll*[66] Sheriff Principal Bowen declined to follow these decisions "because of what I perceive to be the plain terms of the rules,

---

[60] r.9.1(6).
[61] r.9.1(7).
[62] r.9.1(8).
[63] r.11.1(7) and (8).
[64] 1990 S.L.T. (Sh.Ct.) 87.
[65] 1987 S.C.L.R. 332.
[66] 1999 S.L.T. (Sh.Ct.) 23.

the underlying purpose of them, and the potential consequences of applying the 'liberal' interpretation". He said:

> "Read along with the sub-paragraphs which preceded, it is in my view quite apparent that the purpose of the provisions relating to recall of decree are to give a party who has inadvertently allowed decree to pass against him one opportunity, and one opportunity only, to rectify the situation without resort to an appeal. Applying the plain terms of the rules has that effect. If a party lodges a minute for recall of the decree but fails to attend at the hearing to move it the decree will nevertheless be recalled and the case may then be disposed of under the provisions of rule 13. The party would not get a second opportunity to repeat the exercise, although it might be that he could subsequently seek to be relieved of his failure to attend at the hearing by virtue of the relevant dispensing power."

It is submitted that this approach is preferable to that expressed in the earlier cases. As Sheriff Principal Bowen pointed out, if merely lodging a minute to recall does not constitute an application the defender could repeatedly lodge such minutes and prevent enforcement action being taken by the pursuer.

A recall is requested by lodging with the sheriff clerk a minute in Form 20 explaining the party's failure to appear. Where defenders are seeking recall they must also lodge their defences if they have not already done so. Similarly, if pursuers are seeking recall of decrees granted in relation to counterclaims they must lodge their proposed answers.

Normally, a minute for recall must be lodged within 14 days of the grant of the decree. However, where the recall is by a pursuer against a decree which has been granted in relation to a counterclaim, or by a defender, different time limits apply. If the claim has been served outwith the UK as provided in rule 6.5, the minute of recall must be lodged "within a reasonable time after he had knowledge of the decree against him or in any event before the expiring of one year from the date of that decree". In other cases of this kind the time limit is 14 days from the earlier of the execution of a charge or execution of arrestment.

On receiving the minute of recall the sheriff clerk fixes a date, time and place for the hearing of the minute. The party requesting the recall must then serve on the other party a copy of the minute in Form 20a. and a note of the time, date and place of the hearing. Where a party seeking recall is not a partnership, body corporate or represented by a solicitor the sheriff clerk must assist him or her to complete the minute of recall and must arrange service of it. A party who receives notice of the minute of recall must return forthwith to the sheriff clerk any extract the decree which they have. The effect of carrying out this procedure is to prevent the party from taking further action to implement a decree.

At the hearing of the minute of recall "the sheriff shall recall the decree so far as not implemented". This appears to mean that the sheriff has no discretion in the matter and sits oddly with the requirement that the party applying for the recall must provide an explanation for failing to appear originally. The small claim rule is very similar to the reponing rule in ordinary cause procedure, rule 28. Both require an explanation and the stating of a defence. The small claim rule, however, is significantly different in that it states that the sheriff "shall recall" whereas the ordinary cause rules says that he or she "may ... recall the decree". This ordinary cause rule has been authoritatively discussed by a court of five judges in the Inner House in *Forbes v Johnstone*.[67] As Lord President Hope pointed out in giving the judgment of the court, "As for the explanation it is not a requirement of the rules that [the sheriff] must be satisfied that it provides a reasonable excuse for the non-appearance". This would also apply to small claim procedure. Provided that a defence has been stated that is the end of the matter in a small claim. As *Forbes v Johnstone* makes clear, in ordinary cause the sheriff does have a discretion.

When the decree has been recalled the hearing then proceeds as the Hearing referred to in rule 9.1(2). In other words, the claim goes ahead in the normal way.

MISCELLANEOUS MATTERS

Continuations

It is permissible to continue a Hearing though, in a procedure intended to be speedy and inexpensive and to encourage individuals to represent themselves, it is important to restrict this facility to a minimum. It is clearly necessary where the defender has sent a cheque which has still to clear, or where settlement has been agreed but payment has not yet been made. It seems clear that sheriffs ought not to grant continuations to allow representatives to take instructions or to make enquiries.

Sists

Under the original rules there was no provision for sisting an action and the possibility of sisting a party was implied by the incorporation of an

---

[67] 1995 S.C. 220; 1995 S.L.T. 158.

ordinary cause rule relating to the transfer of an action on the death of a party. Both these procedures are now expressly provided for.

Rule 10.2 provides for the possibility of sist in a claim which is to be done by an incidental application. The party seeking the sist must give a reason and this is recorded in the register of small claims and on the summons. Where a claim has been sisted the sheriff may, after giving the parties an opportunity to be heard, recall the sist. The sisting of a small claim is likely to be fairly rare. For one thing, small claim procedure is intended to be expeditious which is inconsistent with sisting. In any event, a common ground for sisting an action in other procedures is to enable a party to apply for legal aid and this is not applicable to small claim procedure for which legal aid is not available. However, a sist can be appropriate where the parties request time to negotiate a settlement. It will be essential in the unlikely event of a reference to the European Court of Justice. Rule 18.4 provides specifically for this situation.

The new rules also make explicit provision for the quite separate sisting of a party. This applies were a party to a claim dies or becomes legally incapable of carrying on the action. Rule 14.1(1) provides that in these circumstances someone claiming to represent that party or his or her estate may apply to be sisted as a party to the claim. This is done by incidental application.

Should no one apply to be sisted as a party in place of the deceased or incapable person rule 14.1(2) deals with the situation. Any other party to the claim may apply by incidental application to have the claim transferred in favour of or against anyone who represents the incapable party or his or her estate.

Incidental applications

There are a number of circumstances in which it may be necessary to make some incidental application in connection with a small claim. The circumstances in which this is appropriate are, in nearly all cases, set out in the rules. An alteration of the summons, form of response, counter-claim or the note of disputed issues may be effected in this way.[68] Leave to enter a claim as an additional defender,[69] to sist a party[70] and to transfer the claim against or in favour of the representative of a deceased or incapable claimant are also done by this method.[71] An application to

---

[68] r.12.1(1).
[69] r.13.1(1).
[70] r.14.1(1).
[71] r.14.1(2).

grant commission and diligence to recover documents,[72] to make a reference to the European Court of Justice[73] and to grant decree in terms of an alternative claim for payment where decree for delivery or recovery of movable property, or implement of an obligation has been granted, are also made by incidental application.[74] The procedure is also used where early extract of a decree is required[75] and where an application in relation to the management of damages on behalf of someone under legal incapacity has to be made.[76] Section 37(2B)(b) of the Sheriff Courts (Scotland) Act 1971 provides that the parties may make a joint motion to remit the claim to summary or ordinary cause. While the rules do not deal with this situation it seems likely that this should be done by incidental application.

Rule 10.1(1) provides that, except where otherwise provided, any incidental application in a small claim may be made in one of two ways. It may be made orally with the leave of the sheriff during any hearing or by lodging a written application with the sheriff clerk. Where the application is lodged in writing it shall only be heard after not less than two days' notice has been given to the other party.[77] An unrepresented private individual may require the sheriff clerk to intimate the application to the other party.[78] Where the party to whom notice of an incidental application has been given intimates to the sheriff clerk and the applicant that the application is not opposed the application need not call in court.[79] The intimation must be made before noon on the day before the application is due to be heard.[80] Rule 5.1(3) requires the sheriff clerk to keep details of incidental applications in the Register of Small Claims.

Rule 10.1, unlike its predecessor (rule 33), makes clear that it is possible to make an incidental application orally. This permits minor amendments to names and addresses on the summons to be made at the Hearing, usually with the consent of both parties.[81] It is usual for an application for a time to pay direction to be made orally. Although there

---

[72] r.17.1(1).
[73] r.18.2(1).
[74] r.21.2(1).
[75] r.21.5(2).
[76] r.24.3(1)(2).
[77] r.10.1(2).
[78] r.10.1(3).
[79] r.10.1(4).
[80] r.10.1(5).
[81] The learned commentator in his note to the report of *Chris Hart (Business Sales) Ltd v Alan Rome*, 1993 S.C.L.R. 147 at 148–149 endorsed the view expressed at p.60 of the 1st edition of this book that it would be unfortunate if two days notice of motions for minor amendments was considered necessary.

is no reference to the use of an incidental application for the similar time order it would seem appropriate to permit an oral application in that case too. In some cases the rule prescribing the use of incidental application procedure expressly provides that proper formality be observed. This is the case where the application is for leave to enter as an additional defender.[82] Where the application is to sist a party or to transfer a claim in favour of or against someone representing a deceased or incapacitated party there is no reference for the need for a written application.[83] It would seem as appropriate in this case as in that for leave to enter as an additional defender. The other situation where the rules require a written application is where decree is sought in terms of an alternative claim for payment where decree for delivery or recovery of movable property, or implement of an obligation has not been complied with.[84]

Interim relief

Circumstances may well arise where a party believes that some kind of interim relief is necessary to preserve the status quo while the small claim is resolved. There is no specific power in the small claims rules to grant interdict. However it may be possible to do so relying on the inherent power of the sheriff. It has already been noted[85] that there is power for the sheriff to regulate all matters relating to interim possession and make other orders pending an appeal. There are wide powers under s.1 of the Administration of Justice (Scotland) Act 1972 to order the inspection, photographing, preservation, custody and detention of documents and other property which appears to the court to be properly as to which any question may relevantly arise in any existing proceedings or in proceedings which are likely to be brought, and to order the production and recovery of such property. The ordinary cause rule providing the detailed procedure to be followed in such cases applies also to summary cause but there is no similar provision in the small claim rules. The primary legislation is not excluded from applying to small claims, and it would seem that it could be applied using the procedure for incidental applications. If this should prove incorrect it is submitted that the same result could be achieved by the exercise by the sheriff of his power at common law to make orders for the preservation of property.[86]

[82] r.13.1.
[83] r.14.1.
[84] r.21.2.
[85] See p.61, above.
[86] See *Macphail* (2nd ed.), Vol.2, para.11–05.

Abandonment

At any time prior to decree being pronounced the pursuer may offer to abandon the small claim.[87] Such an offer could be effected by an incidental application. When an offer to abandon is made, the sheriff clerk assesses the expenses payable by the defender on such basis as the sheriff may direct, subject to s.36B of the Sheriff Courts (Scotland) Act 1971 and rule 21.6.[88] If the pursuer pays the defender's expenses within 14 days of assessment the court will dismiss the claim.[89] If not, the defender is entitled to absolvitor with expenses.[90]

The effect of abandonment is that if an offer to do so is accepted the claim is dismissed. It is, therefore, possible to raise another action on the same facts which would not be possible if a decree of absolvitor had been granted as the issue would be *res judicata*.

The scope for abandonment is probably rather limited in the small claim procedure. One reason for abandoning a claim in other procedures is that the pursuer has a good claim that is proceeding on the wrong legal basis. Given the nature and purpose of the Hearing it seems that there might well be scope to establish the correct legal basis at that Hearing and thus avoid having to seek permission to abandon. The absence of a key witness or the realisation that the claim is worth more than originally thought might be other reasons for seeking abandonment. Given the economics of small claims it seems a route that should probably be avoided except, perhaps, where the claim is worth much more than originally thought and has to be transferred to another procedure.

Reference to the Court of the European Communities

It seems unlikely that there will be many references from small claims procedure to the European Court of Justice. The procedure for such a possibility is set out in Chapter 18 of the rules.

Register of small claims

The sheriff clerk is required by rule 5.1 to keep a Register of Small claims. This records claims and incidental applications made in claims. It may be kept in either electronic or documentary form. The register

---

[87] r.19.1(1).
[88] r.19.1(2).
[89] r.19.1(3).
[90] r.19.1(4).

contains a note of all claims, minutes under rule 22.1 relating to the recall of decrees and details of incidental applications. The entry for each claim or minute must contain the details of the parties to the claim, their representatives, the nature and amount of the claim and its forensic history.[91] Details of any incidental applications must also be recorded including their nature, whether the parties attended the hearing, the names of their representatives and the interlocutor issued or the order made.[92]

On a day when an application in a claim is determined or an order is made the register must be "authenticated in some appropriate manner" by the sheriff.[93] The phraseology takes account of the possibility that the register maybe in electronic form. The register must be open for inspection during normal business hours without charge "to all concerned".[94]

Custody of documents

Documents or other productions which have been referred to or lodged during a hearing shall be retained in the custody of the sheriff clerk until any appeal has been disposed of. After the claim has been disposed of the party who has lodged a production must uplift it within 14 days. If this is not done the sheriff clerk can dispose of it in such manner as the sheriff directs after giving the party or his or her solicitor 28 days' notice of intention to do so.[95]

Documents lost or destroyed

Rule 16.3 deals with the loss or destruction of various documents relating to small claims. These are the summons, the form of response, a counterclaim, the Register of Small Claims and any other document lodged in connection with a claim. It provides that a copy of such a document may be substituted and shall "for the purposes of the cause, including the use of diligence, be equivalent to the original".[96]

---

[91] r.5.1(2).
[92] r.5.1(3).
[93] r.5.1(4)(a).
[94] r.5.1(4)(b).
[95] r.16.4.
[96] r.16.2(3)(b).

Application of rules to solicitors

Where a rule requires something to be done by, or intimated or sent to, a party, it shall be sufficient compliance with the rule if it is done by, or intimated or sent to, the solicitor acting for that party in the small claim.[97]

Dispensing power

Rule 3.1(1) provides that:

> "(1) The sheriff may relieve any party from the consequences of any failure to comply with the provisions of these Rules which is shown to be due to mistake, oversight or other excusable cause, on such terms and conditions as he thinks fit.
>
> (2) Where the sheriff relieves a party from the consequences of the failure to comply with a provision of these Rules under paragraph (1) he may make such order as he thinks to enable the small claim to proceed as if such failure had not occurred."

The rule is similar to the original small claim rule and to the form of the equivalent rules in summary and ordinary cause as well as the Court of Session until recently. The main difference is that the words "other excusable cause" replace "other cause, not being wilful non-observance of the rules". It is thought that this change has little significance as it reflects the meaning given to the original phrase in more than one case.[98] Authoritative guidance from a five judge Inner House in *Grier v Wimpey Plant & Transport Ltd*[99] on the older form of the rule in the ordinary cause procedure is still relevant to the new small claim rule. In that case the Lord Justice Clerk (Ross), delivering the judgment of the court, disapproved of the view of Lord President Clyde in *Grieve v Batchelor and Buckling*[1] that the power should be exercised "only very rarely". He endorsed the more liberal approach of the Inner House in *Dalgety's Trs v Drummond*.[2]

This rule gives the sheriff a wide power and, as it is in the same terms as the previous summary cause power,[3] the observation of Sheriff Principal Caplan is relevant. He said: "In exercising that particular

---

[97] r.4.6.
[98] See *Anderson v British Coal Corp*, 1992 S.L.T. 398 and *Dalgety's Trs v Drummond*, 1938 S.L.T. 495; 1938 S.C. 709.
[99] 1994 S.L.T. 714.
[1] 1961 S.L.T. 151; 1961 S.C. 12.
[2] 1938 S.L.T. 495; 1938 S.C. 709.
[3] Act of Sederunt (Summary Cause Rules, Sheriff Court) 1976, para.5.

power the sheriff has an unqualified discretion and his having regard to the widest interests of justice between the parties can scarcely be said to be inappropriate".[4] In *Alpine House Ltd v Links*[5] Sheriff Principal Hay observed that "The decision on whether or not to exercise the dispensing power in any particular case is a matter within the sheriff's discretion, and is not one with which an appeal court will readily interfere". He refused to interfere where the sheriff had indicated that he would not have exercised the power in favour of a party who had failed to apply for recall of a decree until 42 days after the time limit for doing so had expired.

It has also been considered in a small claim appeal where the defender's solicitor had stated at the preliminary hearing that the sum sued for was due but that she wished the cause to be continued to permit a counterclaim to be lodged. The sheriff pointed out that there was no provision for counterclaims but that it would be competent to bring another small claim to cover the matter intended to be raised by the counterclaim. Decree was then granted, but extract was superseded for three months to give time for the second claim to be disposed of At the appeal it was explained that what should have been stated was that the action would be defended on the ground that there was a right of set-off. Sheriff Principal Ireland refused to invoke the dispensing power. He said:

> "Notwithstanding the wide terms of [the dispensing power], it does not in my view apply to a case like this. It has not been shown that the failure to state the defence was due to mistake or oversight or indeed to any other cause. All that is known is that a defence was not stated. In these circumstances there is no ground for interfering with the sheriff's disposal of the case".[6]

A dispensing power in very similar language is available to Court of Session judges and to sheriffs in ordinary causes, and reference to decisions under those powers may be of assistance. In *Barnes (Flexible Packaging) Ltd v Okhai (Flexible Packaging) Ltd*[7] it was held that the power available to the Court of Session should not be used to give retrospective effect to an amendment of the rules. In *Grier v Wimpey Plant & Transport Ltd* the Inner House held that the court had been in error in *Morton v NL Sperry Sun (UK) Ltd* "when it confined the

[4] *W. Jack Baillie Associates v Kennedy*, 1985 S.L.T. (Sh.Ct.) 53 at 56.
[5] 1990 S.L.T. (Sh.Ct.) 87.
[6] *Slessor v Burnett-Stuart*, 1990 S.L.T. (Sh.Ct.) 62.
[7] 1978 S.L.T. (Notes) 72.

application of the [equivalent] ordinary cause rule ... to cases where there had been a breach of an express obligation laid upon a solicitor". They went on to say that the rule "can be invoked to relieve a party from the consequences of his failure to take any step in terms of the rules which was necessary to make progress in his action".[8] This overruled the narrow approach taken in *Smith v Daram*.[9] The exercise of the dispensing power has been held to be a question of law rather than fact and thus could be the subject of an appeal.[10] In *Miro Windows Ltd v Mrugala*[11] Sheriff Principal Hay followed his own decision in *Alloa Brewing Co Ltd v Parker*[12] and stated that "I am unable to hold that the dispensing power in terms of rule 1 [of the ordinary cause rules] can competently be invoked to recall an extract which had been properly issued and obtained in good faith before the motion to allow the appeal to be heard was lodged." The power cannot be exercised by the sheriff of his own volition[13] at least, to quote Sheriff Principal Hay in *McMillan v Webb*,[14] where the proceedings "were adversarial in nature and in which each party was represented by a solicitor". In small claim procedure this will not always be the case and it leaves open the possibility of the sheriff raising the point to assist unrepresented parties. In *Douglas v Fife Regional Council*[15] it was pointed out that the dispensing power could not be used where the breach of the rules had been by the court.

Correction of interlocutors

Rule 21.4 permits the sheriff, at any time before extract to correct any clerical or incidental error in his interlocutor. "A clerical error is an error made in copying or writing. An incidental error is thought to be one the correction of which would not alter the interlocutor in substance, such as an error in expression."[16]

---

[8] *ibid.* at 719.
[9] 1990 S.L.T. (Sh.Ct.) 94.
[10] *Webster Engineering Services v Gibson*, 1987 S.L.T. (Sh.Ct.) 101.
[11] 1990 S.L.T. (Sh.Ct.) 66.
[12] 1990 S.L.T. (Sh.Ct.) 57.
[13] 1993 S.C.L.R. 147; see also *Chris Hart (Business Sales) Ltd v Rome*, 1993 S.C.L.R. 147.
[14] 1993 S.L.T. (Sh.Ct.) 28.
[15] 1991 S.C.L.R. 521.
[16] Macphail (2nd ed.), Vol.2, para.5–87.

Damages payable to person under disability
Chapter 24, rules 24.1 to 24.4 deals with situations where persons under legal disability, other than those under 18, become entitled to a sum of money as a result of a decree or extra-judicial settlement. Rule 24.1(1) gives the sheriff discretion to make such order regarding the payment and management of the money as he thinks fit. Payment may be made to the Accountant of Court, the guardian of the person under disability or the sheriff clerk for the district where the person under disability lives to be administered by him or her or directly to the person under disability. In practice, where the disability is by reason of insanity there will usually be a curator bonis. Payment will normally be made to him or her.

Where the legal disability is being under the age of 16, rule 24.5 provides that the procedure set out in the Children (Scotland) Act 1995 should be used. Those aged 16 or 17 can give valid receipts for money as a result of the Age of Legal Capacity (Scotland) Act 1991.

PART 2—LEGISLATION

ACT OF SEDERUNT (SMALL CLAIM RULES) 2002

The Lords of Council and Session, under and by virtue of the powers conferred by section 32 of the Sheriff Courts (Scotland) Act 1971 and of all other powers enabling them in that behalf, having approved draft rules submitted to them by the Sheriff Court Rules Council in accordance with section 34 of the said Act of 1971, do hereby enact and declare:

Citation and commencement

1.—(1) This Act of Sederunt may be cited as the Act of Sederunt (Small Claim Rules) 2002 and shall come into force on 10th June 2002.

(2) This Act of Sederunt shall be inserted in the Books of Sederunt.

Small Claim Rules

2. The provisions of Schedule 1 to this Act of Sederunt shall have effect for the purpose of providing rules for the form of summary cause process known as a small claim.

Transitional provision

3. Nothing in Schedule 1 to this Act of Sederunt shall apply to a small claim commenced before 10th June 2002 and any such claim shall proceed according to the law and practice in force immediately before that date.

Revocation

4. The Acts of Sederunt mentioned in column (1) of Schedule 2 to this Act of Sederunt are revoked to the extent specified in column (3) of that Schedule except in relation to any small claim commenced before 10th June 2002.

SCHEDULE 1

Small Claim Rules 2002
Arrangement of Rules

CHAPTER 1

Citation, interpretation and application

Citation, interpretation and application
1.1.—(1) These Rules may be cited as the Small Claim Rules 2002.
   (2) In these rules—

> "the 1971 Act" means the Sheriff Courts (Scotland) Act 1971;
> "the 1975 Act" means the Litigants in Person (Costs and Expenses) Act 1975;
> "authorised lay representative" means a person to whom section 32(1) of the Solicitors (Scotland) Act 1980 (offence to prepare writs) does not apply by virtue of section 32(2)(a) of that Act;
> "small claim" has the meaning assigned to it by section 35(2) of the 1971 Act;
> "summary cause" has the meaning assigned to it by section 35(1) of the 1971 Act.

   (3) Any reference in these Rules to a specified rule shall be construed as a reference to the rule bearing that number in these Rules, and a reference to a specified paragraph, sub-paragraph or head shall be construed as a reference to the paragraph, sub-paragraph or head so numbered or lettered in the provision in which that reference occurs.
   (4) A form referred to by number in these Rules means the form so numbered in Appendix 1 to these rules or a form substantially of the same effect with such variation as circumstances may require.
   (5) The glossary in Appendix 2 to these Rules is a guide to the meaning of certain legal expressions used in these Rules, but is not to be taken as giving those expressions any meaning which they do not have in law generally.
   (6) These Rules shall apply to a small claim.

CHAPTER 2

Representation

Representation
2.1.—(1) A party may be represented by an advocate, solicitor or, subject to paragraph (3), an authorised lay representative.
   (2) An authorised lay representative may in representing a party do everything for the preparation and conduct of a small claim as may be done by an individual conducting his own claim.
   (3) If the sheriff finds that the authorised lay representative is—

   (a) not a suitable person to represent the party; or
   (b) not in fact authorised to do so,

   that person must cease to represent the party.

CHAPTER 3

Relief from failure to comply with Rules

Dispensing power of sheriff
3.1.—(1) The sheriff may relieve any party from the consequences of any failure to comply with the provisions of these Rules which is shown to be due to mistake, oversight or other excusable cause, on such conditions as he thinks fit.

(2) Where the sheriff relieves a party from the consequences of the failure to comply with a provision in these Rules under paragraph (1), he may make such order as he thinks fit to enable the claim to proceed as if the failure to comply with the provision had not occurred.

CHAPTER 4

Commencement of claim

Form of summons
4.1.—(1) A small claim shall be commenced by summons, which shall be in Form 1.

(2) The claim in a small claim summons may be in one of Forms 2 to 4.

Statement of claim
4.2. The pursuer must insert a statement of his claim in the summons to give the defender fair notice of the claim; and the statement must include—

(a) details of the basis of the claim including relevant dates; and
(b) if the claim arises from the supply of goods or services, a description of the goods or services and the date or dates on or between which they were supplied and, where relevant, ordered.

Defender's copy summons
4.3. A copy summons shall be served on the defender—

(a) in Form 1a where—
    (i) the small claim is for, or includes a claim for, payment of money; and
    (ii) an application for a time to pay direction under the Debtors (Scotland) Act 1987 or time order under the Consumer Credit Act 1974 may be applied for; or
(b) in Form 1b in every other case.

Authentication and effect of summons
4.4.—(1) A summons shall be authenticated by the sheriff clerk in some appropriate manner except where—

(a) he refuses to do so for any reason;
(b) the defender's address is unknown; or

(c) a party seeks to alter the normal period of notice specified in rule 4.5(2).

(2) If any of paragraphs (1)(a), (b) or (c) applies, the summons shall be authenticated by the sheriff, if he thinks it appropriate.

(3) The authenticated summons shall be warrant for—

(a) service on the defender; and
(b) where the appropriate warrant has been sought in the summons—
    (i) arrestment on the dependence; or
    (ii) arrestment to found jurisdiction,
    as the case may be.

Period of notice

4.5.—(1) A claim shall proceed after the appropriate period of notice of the summons has been given to the defender prior to the return day.

(2) The appropriate period of notice shall be—

(a) 21 days where the defender is resident or has a place of business within Europe; or
(b) 42 days where the defender is resident or has a place of business outwith Europe.

(3) The sheriff may, on cause shown, shorten or extend the period of notice on such conditions as to the form of service as he may direct, but in any case where the period of notice is reduced at least two days' notice must be given.

(4) If a period of notice expires on a Saturday, Sunday, public or court holiday, the period of notice shall be deemed to expire on the next day on which the sheriff clerk's office is open for civil court business.

(5) Notwithstanding the terms of section 4(2) of the Citation Amendment (Scotland) Act 1882, where service is by post the period of notice shall run from the beginning of the day next following the date of posting.

(6) The sheriff clerk shall insert in the summons—

(a) the return day, which is the last day on which the defender may return a form of response to the sheriff clerk; and
(b) the hearing date, which is the date set for the hearing of the claim.

Intimation

4.6. Any provision in these Rules requiring papers to be sent to or any intimation to be made to any party or applicant shall be construed as if the reference to the party or applicant included a reference to the solicitor representing that party or applicant.

CHAPTER 5

Register of Small Claims

Register of Small Claims

5.1.—(1) The sheriff clerk shall keep a register of claims and incidental applications made in claims, which shall be known as the Register of Small Claims.

(2) There shall be entered in the Register of Small Claims a note of all claims, together with a note of all minutes under rule 22.1(1) (recall of decree) and the entry for each claim or minute must contain the following particulars where appropriate—

(a) the names, designations and addresses of the parties;
(b) whether the parties were present or absent at any hearing, including an inspection, and the names of their representatives;
(c) the nature of the claim;
(d) the amount of any claim;
(e) the date of issue of the summons;
(f) the method of service;
(g) the return day;
(h) the hearing date;
(i) whether a form of response was lodged and details of it;
(j) the period of notice if shortened or extended in accordance with rule 4.5(3);
(k) details of any minute by the pursuer regarding a time to pay direction or time order, or minute by the pursuer requesting decree or other order;
(l) details of any interlocutors issued;
(m) details of the final decree and the date of it; and
(n) details of any variation or recall of a decree by virtue of the Debtors (Scotland) Act 1987.

(3) There shall be entered in the Register of Small Claims, in the entry for the claim to which they relate, details of incidental applications including, where appropriate—

(a) whether parties are present or absent at the hearing of the application, and the names of their representatives;
(b) the nature of the application; and
(c) the interlocutor issued or order made.

(4) The Register of Small Claims must be—

(a) authenticated in some appropriate manner by the sheriff in respect of each day any order is made or application determined in a claim; and
(b) open for inspection during normal business hours to all concerned without fee.

(5) The Register of Small Claims may be kept in electronic or documentary form.

CHAPTER 6

Service and return of the summons

Persons carrying on business under trading or descriptive name
6.1.—(1) A person carrying on a business under a trading or descriptive name may sue or be sued in such trading or descriptive name alone.

(2) An extract of a decree pronounced in a claim against such person under such trading or descriptive name shall be a valid warrant for diligence against that person.

(3) A summons, decree, charge or other document following upon such summons or decree in a claim in which a person carrying on business under a trading or descriptive name sues or is sued in that name may be served—

(a) at any place of business or office at which such business is carried on within the sheriffdom of the sheriff court in which the claim is brought; or

(b) if there is no place of business within that sheriffdom, at any place where such business is carried on (including the place of business or office of the clerk or secretary of any company, corporation or association or firm).

Form of service

6.2.—(1) Subject to rule 6.6 (service where address of defender is unknown), a form of service in Form 5 must be enclosed with the defender's copy summons.

(2) After service has been effected a certificate of execution of service in Form 6 must be prepared and signed by the person effecting service.

(3) When service is effected by a sheriff officer the certificate of execution of service must specify whether the service was personal or, if otherwise, the mode of service and the name of any person to whom the defender's copy summons was delivered.

(4) If service is effected in accordance with rule 6.4(2) (service within Scotland by sheriff officer where personal service etc. unsuccessful) the certificate must also contain a statement of—

(a) the mode of service previously attempted; and

(b) the circumstances which prevented the service from being effected.

Service of the summons

6.3.—(1) Subject to rule 6.5 (service on persons outwith Scotland), a copy summons may be served on the defender—

(a) by the pursuer's solicitor, a sheriff officer or the sheriff clerk sending it by first class recorded delivery post; or

(b) in accordance with rule 6.4 (service within Scotland by sheriff officer).

(2) On the face of the envelope used for postal service in terms of this rule, there must be printed or written a notice in Form 7.

(3) The certificate of execution of service in the case of postal service must have annexed to it any relevant postal receipt.

(4) If the pursuer requires the sheriff clerk to effect service on his behalf by virtue of section 36A of the 1971 Act (pursuer not being a partnership, body corporate or acting in a representative capacity) under paragraph (1), he may require the sheriff clerk to supply him with a copy of the summons.

Service within Scotland by sheriff officer

6.4.—(1) A sheriff officer may validly serve any summons, decree, charge or other document following upon such summons or decree issued in a claim by—

(a) personal service; or

(b) leaving it in the hands of—

    (i) an inmate at the person's dwelling place; or

    (ii) an employee at the person's place of business.

(2) If a sheriff officer has been unsuccessful in effecting service in accordance with paragraph (1), he may, after making diligent inquiries, serve the document—

(a) by depositing it in the person's dwelling place or place of business by means of a letter box or by other lawful means; or

(b) by affixing it to the door of the person's dwelling place or place of business.

(3) If service is effected in accordance with paragraph (2), the sheriff officer must thereafter send by ordinary post to the address at which he thinks it most likely that the person may be found a letter containing a copy of the document.

(4) In proceedings in or following on a claim, it shall be necessary for any sheriff officer to be accompanied by a witness except where service, citation or intimation is to be made by post.

(5) Where the firm which employs the sheriff officer has in its possession—

(a) the document or a copy of it certified as correct by the pursuer's solicitor or the sheriff clerk, the sheriff officer may serve the document upon the defender without having the document or certified copy in his possession (in which case he shall if required to do so by the person on whom service is executed and within a reasonable time of being so required, show the document or certified copy to the person); or

(b) a certified copy of the interlocutor pronounced allowing service of the document, the sheriff officer may serve the document without having in his possession the certified copy interlocutor if he has in his possession a facsimile copy of the certified copy interlocutor (which he shall show, if required, to the person on whom service is executed).

(6) If the pursuer requires the sheriff clerk to effect service of the summons on his behalf by virtue of section 36A of the 1971 Act, the sheriff clerk may instruct a sheriff officer to effect service in accordance with this rule on payment to the sheriff clerk by the pursuer of the fee prescribed by order of the Scottish Ministers.

Service on persons outwith Scotland

6.5.—(1) If any summons, decree, charge or other document following upon such summons or decree, or any charge or warrant, requires to be served outwith Scotland on any person, it must be served in accordance with this rule.

(2) If the person has a known home or place of business in—

(a) England and Wales, Northern Ireland, the Isle of Man or the Channel Islands; or

(b) any country with which the United Kingdom does not have a convention providing for service of writs in that country,

the document must be served either—

(i) by posting in Scotland a copy of the document in question in a registered letter addressed to the person at his residence or place of business; or

(ii) in accordance with the rules for personal service under the domestic law of the place in which the document is to be served.

(3) Subject to paragraph (4), if the document requires to be served in a country which is a party to the Hague Convention on the Service Abroad of Judicial and Extra-Judicial Documents in Civil or Commercial Matters dated 15th November 1965 or the European Convention on Jurisdiction and Enforcement of Judgments in Civil and Commercial Matters as set out in Schedule 1 or 3C to the Civil Jurisdiction and Judgments Act 1982, it must be served—

(a) by a method prescribed by the internal law of the country where service is to be effected for the service of documents in domestic actions upon persons who are within its territory;

(b) by or through a British consular authority at the request of the Secretary of State for Foreign and Commonwealth Affairs;

(c) by or through a central authority in the country where service is to be effected at the requested of the Secretary of State for Foreign and Commonwealth Affairs;

(d) where the law of the country in which the person resides permits, by posting in Scotland a copy of the document in a registered letter addressed to the person at his residence; or

(e) where the law of the country in which service is to be effected permits, service by an huissier, other judicial officer or competent official of the country where service is to be made.

(4) If the document requires to be served in a country to which Council Regulation (EC) No. 1348/2000 on the service in the Member States of judicial and extrajudicial documents in civil or commercial matters applies, service may be effected by a method prescribed in paragraph (3)(b) or (c) only in exceptional circumstances.

(5) If the document requires to be served in a country with which the United Kingdom has a convention on the service of writs in that country other than the conventions specified in paragraph (3) or the regulation specified in paragraph (4), it must be served by one of the methods approved in the relevant convention.

(6) Subject to paragraph (9), a document which requires to be posted in Scotland for the purposes of this rule must be posted by a solicitor, the sheriff clerk or a sheriff officer, and the form for service and the certificate of execution of service must be in Forms 5 and 6 respectively.

(7) On the face of the envelope used for postal service under this rule there must be written or printed a notice in Form 7.

(8) Where service is effected by a method specified in paragraph (3)(b) or (c), the pursuer must—

(a) send a copy of the summons and warrant for service with form of service attached, or other document, with a request for service to be effected by the method indicated in the request to the Secretary of State for Foreign and Commonwealth Affairs; and

(b) lodge in process a certificate of execution of service signed by the authority which has effected service.

(9) If service is effected by the method specified in paragraph (3)(c), the pursuer must—

(a) send to the official in the country in which service is to be effected a copy of the summons and warrant for service, with citation attached, or other document, with a request for service to be effected by delivery to the defender or his residence; and

(b) lodge in process a certificate of execution of service by the official who has effected service.

(10) Where service is executed in accordance with paragraph (2)(b)(ii) or (3)(a) other than on another party in—

(a) the United Kingdom;

(b) the Isle of Man; or

(c) the Channel Islands,

the party executing service must lodge a certificate stating that the form of service employed is in accordance with the law of the place where the service was executed.

(11) A certificate lodged in accordance with paragraph (10) shall be given by a person who is conversant with the law of the country concerned and who—

(a) practises or has practised law in that country; or

(b) is a duly accredited representative of the government of that country.

(12) Every summons or document and every citation and notice on the face of the envelope referred to in paragraph (7) must be accompanied by a translation in an official language of the country in which service is to be executed, unless English is an official language of that country.

(13) A translation referred to in paragraph (12) must be certified as a correct translation by the person making it and the certificate must contain the full name, address and qualifications of the translator and be lodged along with the execution of such service.

(14) If the pursuer requires the sheriff clerk to effect service on his behalf under this rule by virtue of section 36A of the 1971 Act (pursuer not a partnership, body corporate or acting in a representative capacity)—

(a) the cost must be borne by the pursuer;

(b) no service shall be instructed by the sheriff clerk until such cost has been paid to him by the pursuer; and

(c) the pursuer may require the sheriff clerk to supply him with a copy of the summons.

Service where address of defender is unknown

6.6.—(1) If the defender's address is unknown to the pursuer and cannot reasonably be ascertained by him, the sheriff may grant warrant to serve the summons—

(a) by the publication of an advertisement in Form 8 in a newspaper circulating in the area of the defender's last known address; or

(b) by displaying on the walls of court a copy of a notice in Form 9.

(2) Where a summons is served in accordance with paragraph (1), the period of notice, which must be fixed by the sheriff, shall run from the date of publication of the advertisement or display on the walls of court, as the case may be.

(3) If service is to be effected under paragraph (1), the pursuer must lodge a defender's copy summons with the sheriff clerk.

(4) The defender may uplift from the sheriff clerk the copy summons lodged in accordance with paragraph (3).

(5) If the pursuer requires the sheriff clerk to effect service on his behalf under paragraph (1) by virtue of section 36A of the 1971 Act (pursuer not a partnership, body corporate or acting in a representative capacity)—

(a) the cost of any advertisement required under sub-paragraph (a) of that paragraph must be borne by the pursuer;

(b) no advertisement required under sub-paragraph (a) of that paragraph shall be instructed by the sheriff clerk until such cost has been paid to him by the pursuer; and

(c) the pursuer may require the sheriff clerk to supply him with a copy of the summons.

(6) A copy of the newspaper containing the advertisement referred to in paragraph (1)(a) must be lodged with the sheriff clerk unless the sheriff clerk instructed such advertisement.

(7) If display on the walls of court is required under paragraph (1)(b), the pursuer must supply to the sheriff clerk for that purpose a completed copy of Form 9.

(8) If service has been made under this rule and thereafter the defender's address becomes known, the sheriff may allow the summons to be amended and, if appropriate, grant warrant for re-service subject to such conditions as he thinks fit.

Endorsation by sheriff clerk of defender's residence not necessary

6.7. Any summons, decree, charge or other document following upon a summons or decree may be served, enforced or otherwise lawfully executed in Scotland without endorsation by a sheriff clerk and, if executed by a sheriff officer, may be so executed by a sheriff officer of the court which granted the summons, or by a sheriff officer of the sheriff court district in which it is to be executed.

Contents of envelope containing defender's copy summons

6.8. Nothing must be included in the envelope containing a defender's copy summons except—

(a) the copy summons;

(b) a response or other notice in accordance with these Rules; and

(c) any other document approved by the sheriff principal.

Re-service

6.9.—(1) If it appears to the sheriff that there has been any failure or irregularity in service upon a defender, the sheriff may order the pursuer to re-serve the summons on such conditions as he thinks fit.

(2) If re-service has been ordered in accordance with paragraph (1) or rule 6.6(8), the claim shall proceed thereafter as if it were a new claim.

Defender appearing barred from objecting to service

6.10.—(1) A person who appears in any claim shall not be entitled to state any objection to the regularity of the execution of service or intimation on him and his appearance shall remedy any defect in such service or intimation.

(2) Nothing in paragraph (1) shall preclude a party pleading that the court has no jurisdiction.

Return of summons and execution

6.11.—(1) If—

(a) someone other than the sheriff clerk has served the summons; and

(b) the case requires to call in court for any reason on the hearing date,

the pursuer must return the summons and the certificate of execution of service to the sheriff clerk at least two days before the hearing date.

(2) If the case does not require to call in court on the hearing date, the pursuer must return the certificate of execution of service to the sheriff clerk by the date mentioned in paragraph (1) above.

(3) If the pursuer fails to return the summons or certificate of execution of service in accordance with paragraph (1) or (2) as appropriate, the sheriff may dismiss the claim.

CHAPTER 7

Arrestment

Service of schedule of arrestment
7.1. If a schedule of arrestment has not been personally served on an arrestee, the arrestment shall have effect only if a copy of the schedule is also sent by registered post or the first class recorded delivery service to—

(a) the last known place of residence of the arrestee; or
(b) if such place of residence is not known, or if the arrestee is a firm or corporation, to the arrestee's principal place of business if known, or, if not known, to any known place of business of the arrestee,

and the sheriff officer must, on the certificate of execution, certify that this has been done and specify the address to which the copy of the schedule was sent.

Arrestment before service
7.2.—(1) An arrestment to found jurisdiction or an arrestment on the dependence of a claim used prior to service shall cease to have effect, unless the summons is served within 21 days from the date of execution of the arrestment.

(2) When such an arrestment as is referred to in paragraph (1) has been executed, the party using it must forthwith report the execution to the sheriff clerk.

Recall and restriction of arrestment
7.3.—(1) The sheriff may order that an arrestment on the dependence of a claim or counterclaim shall cease to have effect if the party whose funds or property are arrested—

(a) pays into court; or
(b) finds caution to the satisfaction of the sheriff clerk in respect of,

the sum claimed together with the sum of £50 in respect of expenses.

(2) Without prejudice to paragraph (1), a party whose funds or property are arrested may at any time apply to the sheriff to exercise his powers to recall or restrict an arrestment on the dependence of a claim or counterclaim, with or without consignation or caution.

(3) An application made under paragraph (3) must be intimated by the applicant to the party who instructed the arrestment.

(4) On payment into court or the finding of caution to the satisfaction of the sheriff clerk in accordance with paragraph (1), or if the sheriff recalls or restricts an arrestment on

the dependence of a claim in accordance with paragraph (2) and any condition imposed by the sheriff has been complied with, the sheriff clerk must—

(a) issue to the party whose funds or property are arrested a certificate in Form 10 authorising the release of any sum or property arrested to the extent ordered by the sheriff; and

(b) send a copy of the certificate to—
    (i) the party who instructed the arrestment; and
    (ii) the party who has possession of the funds or property that are arrested.

CHAPTER 8

Undefended claim

Undefended claim
8.1.—(1) Where the defender has not lodged a form of response on or before the return day, the claim shall not require to call in court.

(2) Where paragraph (1) applies, the pursuer must lodge a minute in Form 11 before the sheriff clerk's office closes for business on the second day before the date set for the hearing.

(3) Where the pursuer has lodged a minute in accordance with paragraph (2), the sheriff may grant decree or other competent order sought in terms of that minute.

(4) Where the pursuer has not lodged a minute in accordance with paragraph (2), the sheriff must dismiss the claim.

Application for time to pay direction or time order
8.2.—(1) If the defender admits the claim, he may, where competent—

(a) make an application for a time to pay direction (including, where appropriate, an application for recall or restriction of an arrestment) or a time order by completing the appropriate parts of the Form 1a and lodging it with the sheriff clerk on or before the return day; or

(b) lodge a form of response indicating that he admits the claim and intends to apply orally for a time to pay direction (including, where appropriate, an application for recall or restriction of an arrestment) or time order.

(2) Where the defender has lodged an application in terms of paragraph (1)(a), the pursuer may intimate that he does not object to the application by lodging a minute in Form 12 before the time the sheriff clerk's office closes for business on the day occurring two days before the hearing date stating that he does not object to the defender's application and seeking decree.

(3) If the pursuer intimates in accordance with paragraph (2) that he does not object to the application—

(a) the sheriff may grant decree on the hearing date;
(b) the parties need not attend; and
(c) the action will not call in court.

(4) If the pursuer wishes to oppose the application for a time to pay direction or time order made in accordance with paragraph (1)(a), he must lodge a minute in Form 13

before the time the sheriff clerk's office closes for business on the day occurring two days before the hearing date.

(5) Where the pursuer objects to an application in terms of paragraph (1)(a) or the defender has lodged a form of response in accordance with paragraph (1)(b), the action shall call in court on the hearing date when the parties may appear and the sheriff must decide the application and grant decree accordingly.

(6) The sheriff shall decide an application in accordance with paragraph (5) whether or not any of the parties appear.

(7) Where the defender has lodged an application in terms of paragraph (1)(a) and the pursuer fails to proceed in accordance with either of paragraphs (2) or (4) the sheriff may dismiss the claim.

Decree in claims to which the Hague Convention or the Civil Jurisdiction and Judgments Act 1982 apply

8.3.—(1) If the summons has been served in a country to which the Hague Convention on the Service Abroad of Judicial and Extra-Judicial Documents in Civil or Commercial Matters dated 15th November 1965 applies, decree must not be granted until it is established to the satisfaction of the sheriff that the requirements of Article 15 of that Convention have been complied with.

(2) Where a defender is domiciled in another part of the United Kingdom or in another Contracting State, the sheriff shall not grant decree until it has been shown that the defender has been able to receive the summons in sufficient time to arrange his defence or that all necessary steps have been taken to that end.

(3) For the purposes of paragraph (2)—

(a) the question whether a person is domiciled in another part of the United Kingdom shall be determined in accordance with sections 41 and 42 of the Civil Jurisdiction and Judgments Act 1982;

(b) the question whether a person is domiciled in another Contracting State shall be determined in accordance with Article 52 of the Convention in Schedule 1 or 3C to that Act; and

(c) the term "Contracting State" has the meaning assigned in section 1 of that Act.

CHAPTER 9

Defended claim

The Hearing

9.1.—(1) Where a defender intends to—

(a) challenge the jurisdiction of the court;

(b) state a defence (including, where appropriate, a counterclaim); or

(c) dispute the amount of the claim,

he must complete the form of response part of Form 1a or 1b as appropriate indicating that intention and lodge it with the sheriff clerk on or before the return day.

(2) Where the defender has lodged a form of response in accordance with paragraph (1) the claim will call in court for a hearing ("the Hearing").

(3) The Hearing shall be held on the hearing date which shall be seven days after the return day.

(4) If the claim is not resolved at the Hearing, the sheriff may continue the Hearing to such other date as he considers to be appropriate.

(5) The defender must attend or be represented at the Hearing and the sheriff shall note any challenge, defence or dispute, as the case may be, on the summons.

(6) Where at the Hearing the defender—

(a) does not appear or is not represented; and
(b) the pursuer is present or is represented,

decree may be granted against the defender in terms of the summons.

(7) Where at the Hearing—

(a) the pursuer does not appear or is not represented; and
(b) the defender is present or represented,

the sheriff may grant decree of dismissal.

(8) If all parties fail to appear at the Hearing, the sheriff shall, unless sufficient reason appears to the contrary, dismiss the claim.

Purpose of the Hearing

9.2.—(1) If, at the Hearing, the sheriff is satisfied that the claim is incompetent or that there is a patent defect of jurisdiction, he must grant decree of dismissal in favour of the defender or, if appropriate, transfer the claim in terms of rule 15.1(2).

(2) At the Hearing, the sheriff shall—

(a) ascertain the factual basis of the claim and any defence, and the legal basis on which the claim and defence are proceeding; and
(b) seek to negotiate and secure settlement of the claim between the parties.

(3) If the sheriff cannot secure settlement of the claim between the parties, he shall—

(a) identify and note on the summons the issues of fact and law which are in dispute;
(b) note on the summons any facts which are agreed; and
(c) if possible reach a decision on the whole dispute on the basis of the information before him.

(4) Where evidence requires to be led for the purposes of reaching a decision on the dispute, the sheriff shall—

(a) direct parties to lead evidence on the disputed issues of fact which he has noted on the summons;
(b) indicate to the parties the matters of fact that require to be proved, and may give guidance on the nature of the evidence to be led; and
(c) fix a hearing on evidence for a later date for that purpose.

Conduct of hearings

9.3.—(1) Any hearing in a claim shall be conducted in accordance with the following paragraphs of this rule.

(2) A hearing shall be conducted as informally as the circumstances of the claim permit.

(3) The procedure to be adopted at a hearing shall be such as the sheriff considers—

(a) to be fair;

(b) best suited to the clarification and determination of the issues before him; and

(c) gives each party sufficient opportunity to present his case.

(4) Before proceeding to hear evidence, the sheriff shall explain to the parties the form of procedure which he intends to adopt.

(5) Having considered the circumstances of the parties and whether (and to what extent) they are represented, the sheriff—

(a) may, in order to assist resolution of the disputed issues of fact, put questions to parties and to witnesses; and

(b) shall (if he considers it necessary for the fair conduct of the hearing) explain any legal terms or expressions which are used.

(6) Evidence will normally be taken on oath or affirmation but the sheriff may dispense with that requirement if it appears reasonable to do so.

Inspection of places and objects

9.4.—(1) If, at any hearing, a disputed issue noted by the sheriff is the quality or condition of an object, the sheriff may inspect the object in the presence of the parties or their representatives in court or, if it is not practicable to bring the object to court, at the place where the object is located.

(2) The sheriff may, if he considers it appropriate, inspect any place that is material to the disputed issues in the presence of the parties or their representatives.

Remit to determine matter of fact

9.5.—(1) The sheriff may, where parties agree, remit to any suitable person to report on any matter of fact.

(2) Where a remit is made under paragraph (1) above, the report of such person shall be final and conclusive with respect to the matter of fact which is the subject of the remit.

(3) A remit shall not be made under paragraph (1) of this rule unless parties have previously agreed the basis upon which the fees, if any, of such person shall be met.

Noting of evidence

9.6. The sheriff must make notes of the evidence at a hearing for his own use and must retain these notes until after any appeal has been disposed of.

Application for time to pay direction or time order in defended claim

9.7. A defender in a claim which proceeds as defended may, where it is competent to do so, make an incidental application or apply orally at any hearing, at any time before decree is granted, for a time to pay direction (including where appropriate, an order recalling or restricting an arrestment on the dependence) or a time order.

Pronouncement of decision

9.8.—(1) The sheriff must, where practicable, give his decision and a brief statement of his reasons at the end of the hearing of a claim, or he may reserve judgment.

(2) If the sheriff reserves judgment, he must, within 28 days of the hearing, give his decision in writing together with a brief note of his reasons, and the sheriff clerk must send a copy to the parties.

(3) After giving his judgment, the sheriff must—

(a) deal with the question of expenses and, where appropriate, make an award of expenses; and

(b) grant decree as appropriate.

(4) The decree of the sheriff shall be a final decree.

CHAPTER 10

Incidental applications and sists

General

10.1.—(1) Except where otherwise provided, any incidental application in a claim may be made—

(a) orally with the leave of the sheriff during any hearing of the claim; or

(b) by lodging the application in written form with the sheriff clerk.

(2) An application lodged in accordance with paragraph (1)(b) may only be heard after not less than two days' notice has been given to the other party.

(3) A party who is not—

(a) a partnership or a body corporate; or

(b) acting in a representative capacity,

and is not represented by a solicitor, may require the sheriff clerk to intimate to the other party a copy of an incidental application.

(4) Where the party receiving notice of an incidental application lodged in accordance with paragraph (1)(b) intimates to the sheriff clerk and the party making the application that it is not opposed, the application shall not require to call in court unless the sheriff so directs.

(5) Any intimation under paragraph (4) shall be made not later than noon on the day before the application is due to be heard.

Application to sist claim

10.2.—(1) Where an incidental application to sist a claim is made, the reason for the sist—

(a) shall be stated by the party seeking the sist; and

(b) shall be recorded in the Register of Small Claims and on the summons.

(2) Where a claim has been sisted, the sheriff may, after giving parties an opportunity to be heard, recall the sist.

CHAPTER 11

Counterclaim

Counterclaim
11.1.—(1) If a defender intends to state a counterclaim he must—

(a) indicate that on the form of response; and
(b) state the counterclaim—
    (i) in writing on the form of response; or
    (ii) orally at the Hearing.

(2) Where a defender states a counterclaim in accordance with paragraph (1)(b)(i) he must at the same time send a copy of the form of response to—

(a) the pursuer; and
(b) any other party.

(3) Where a counterclaim stated in accordance with paragraph (1)(b)(i) seeks warrant for arrestment on the dependence or arrestment to found jurisdiction—

(a) the sheriff clerk may authenticate it in some appropriate manner; or
(b) the defender may apply at the Hearing for the warrant to be authenticated, and the authenticated warrant shall be warrant for—
    (i) arrestment on the dependence; or
    (ii) arrestment to found jurisdiction,
    as the case may be.

(4) Where the sheriff clerk refuses to authenticate a warrant on a counterclaim in accordance with paragraph (3)(a) for any reason, the sheriff may authenticate it.

(5) Where a defender has indicated in terms of paragraph (1)(a) that he intends to state a counterclaim orally at the Hearing the sheriff may continue the Hearing to allow an answer to the counterclaim to be stated.

(6) The defender may state a counterclaim after—

(a) the Hearing; or
(b) any continuation of the Hearing,

as the case may be, only with the leave of the sheriff.

(7) If a counterclaim has been stated orally at any hearing at which the pursuer fails to appear or be represented the sheriff may continue that hearing after noting the counterclaim and the factual basis of it to allow the pursuer to appear.

(8) Intimation of a continued hearing fixed under paragraph (7) shall be given to the pursuer by the sheriff clerk in Form 14 advising him that if he fails to appear or be

represented at the continued hearing decree may be granted in terms of the counter-claim.

CHAPTER 12

Alteration of summons etc.

Alteration of summons etc.
12.1.—(1) The sheriff may, on the incidental application of a party allow amendment of the summons, form of response or any counterclaim, and adjust the note of disputed issues at any time before final judgment is pronounced on the merits.

(2) In an undefended claim, the sheriff may order the amended summons to be re-served on the defender on such period of notice as he thinks fit.

CHAPTER 13

Additional defender

Additional defender
13.1.—(1) Any person who has not been called as a defender may apply by incidental application to the sheriff for leave to enter a claim as a defender, and to state a defence.

(2) An application under this rule must specify—

(a) the applicant's title and interest to enter the claim; and
(b) the grounds of the defence which he proposes to state.

(3) On the lodging of an application under this rule—

(a) the sheriff must fix a date for hearing the application; and
(b) the applicant must forthwith serve a copy of the application and of the order for a hearing on the parties to the claim.

(4) After hearing the applicant and any party to the claim the sheriff may, if he is satisfied that the applicant has shown title and interest to enter the claim, grant the application.

(5) Where an application is granted under paragraph (4)—

(a) the applicant shall be treated as a defender; and
(b) the claim shall proceed against him as if it was the Hearing in terms of rule 9.2.

CHAPTER 14

Applications for sist of party and transference

Application for sist of party and transference
14.1.—(1) If a party dies or becomes legally incapacitated while a claim is depending, any person claiming to represent that party or his estate may apply by incidental application to be sisted as a party to the claim.

(2) If a party dies or becomes legally incapacitated while a claim is depending and the provisions of paragraph (1) are not invoked, any other party may apply by incidental application to have the claim transferred in favour of or against, as the case may be, any person who represents that party or his estate.

CHAPTER 15

Transfer and remit of claims

Transfer to another court

15.1.—(1) The sheriff may transfer a claim to any other sheriff court, whether in the same sheriffdom or not, if the sheriff considers it expedient to do so.

(2) If the sheriff is satisfied that the court has no jurisdiction, he may transfer the claim to any sheriff court in which it appears to the sheriff that it ought to have been brought.

(3) A claim so transferred shall proceed in all respects as if it had been brought originally in the court to which it is transferred.

Remit between procedures

15.2.—(1) If the sheriff makes a direction that a claim is to be treated as an ordinary cause, he must, at the time of making that direction—

(a) direct the pursuer to lodge an initial writ, and intimate it to every other party, within 14 days of the date of the direction;

(b) direct the defender to lodge defences within 28 days of the date of the direction; and

(c) fix a date and time for an Options Hearing and that date shall be the first suitable court day occurring not sooner than ten weeks, or such lesser period as he considers appropriate, after the last date for lodging the initial writ.

(2) If the sheriff directs that a claim is to be treated as a summary cause he must specify the next step of procedure to be followed.

(3) If the sheriff directs that an ordinary cause or a summary cause is to be treated as a claim under these rules it shall call for the Hearing held in terms of rule 9.1(2).

CHAPTER 16

Productions and documents

Lodging of productions

16.1.—(1) A party who intends to rely at a hearing at which evidence is to be led, upon any documents or articles in his possession, which are reasonably capable of being lodged with the court, must—

(a) lodge them with the sheriff clerk together with a list detailing the items no later than 14 days before the hearing; and

(b) at the same time send a copy of the list to the other party.

(2) The documents referred to in paragraph (1) include any affidavit or other written statement admissible under section 2(1) of the Civil Evidence (Scotland) Act 1988.

(3) Subject to paragraph (4), only documents or articles produced—

(a) in accordance with paragraph (1);
(b) at an earlier hearing; or
(c) under rule 17.2(3) or (4),

may be used or put in evidence.

(4) Documents other than those mentioned in paragraph (3) may be used or put in evidence only with the—

(a) consent of the parties; or
(b) permission of the sheriff on cause shown, and on such terms as to expenses or otherwise as to him seem proper.

Borrowing of productions

16.2.—(1) Any productions borrowed must be returned not later than noon on the day preceding the date of any hearing.

(2) A receipt for any production borrowed must be entered in the list of productions and that list must be retained by the sheriff clerk.

(3) Subject to paragraph (4), productions may be borrowed only by—

(a) a solicitor; or
(b) his authorised clerk for whom he shall be responsible.

(4) A party litigant or an authorised lay representative may borrow a production only with permission of the sheriff and subject to such conditions as the sheriff may impose.

(5) Productions may be inspected within the office of the sheriff clerk during normal business hours, and copies may be obtained by a party litigant, where practicable, from the sheriff clerk.

Documents lost or destroyed

16.3.—(1) This rule applies to any—

(a) summons;
(b) form of response;
(c) counterclaim;
(d) Register of Small Claims; or
(e) other document lodged with the sheriff clerk in connection with a claim.

(2) Where any document mentioned in paragraph (1) is—

(a) lost; or
(b) destroyed,

a copy of it, authenticated in such manner as the sheriff may require, may be substituted and shall, for the purposes of the claim including the use of diligence, be equivalent to the original.

Documents and productions to be retained in custody of sheriff clerk

16.4.—(1) This rule applies to all documents or other productions which have at any time been lodged or referred to during a hearing.

(2) The sheriff clerk must retain in his custody any document or other production mentioned in paragraph (1) until—

(a) after the expiry of the period during which an appeal is competent; and
(b) any appeal lodged has been disposed of.

(3) Each party who has lodged productions in a claim shall—

(a) after the final determination of the claim, where no appeal has been lodged, within 14 days after the appeal period has expired; or
(b) within 14 days after the disposal of any appeal lodged on the final determination of the claim,

uplift the productions from the sheriff clerk.

(4) Where any production has not been uplifted as required by paragraph (3), the sheriff clerk shall intimate to—

(a) the solicitor who lodged the production; or
(b) where no solicitor is acting, the party himself or such other party as seems appropriate,

that if he fails uplift the production within 28 days after the date of such intimation, it will be disposed of in such manner as the sheriff directs.

CHAPTER 17

Recovery of documents and attendance of witnesses

Diligence for recovery of documents

17.1.—(1) At any time after a summons has been served, a party may make an incidental application in writing to the sheriff to grant commission and diligence to recover documents.

(2) A party who makes an application in accordance with paragraph (1) must list in the application the documents which he wishes to recover.

(3) The sheriff may grant commission and diligence to recover those documents in the list mentioned in paragraph (2) which he considers relevant to the claim.

Optional procedure before executing commission and diligence

17.1.—(1) Any party who has obtained a commission and diligence for the recovery of documents may, at any time before executing it, serve by first class recorded delivery post on the person from whom the documents are sought to be recovered (or on his known solicitor or solicitors) an order with certificate attached in Form 15.

(2) If in a claim the party in whose favour the commission and diligence has been granted is not—

(a) a partnership or body corporate; or
(b) acting in a representative capacity,

and is not represented by a solicitor, service under paragraph (1) must be effected by the sheriff clerk posting a copy of the order together with a certificate in Form 15 by first class recorded delivery post or, on payment of the fee prescribed by the Scottish Ministers by order, by sheriff officer.

(3) Documents recovered in response to an order under paragraph (1) must be sent to, and retained by, the sheriff clerk who shall, on receiving them, advise the parties that the documents are in his possession and may be examined within his office during normal business hours.

(4) If the party who served the order is not satisfied that—

(a) full production has been made under the specification; or

(b) that adequate reasons for non-production have been given,

he may execute the commission and diligence in normal form, notwithstanding his adoption in the first instance of the procedure in paragraph (1) above.

(5) Documents recovered under this rule may be submitted as evidence at any hearing without further formality, and rule 17.3(3) and (4) shall apply to such documents.

Confidentiality of documents

17.3.—(1) In any claim where a party has obtained a commission and diligence to recover documents and the documents have been produced either—

(a) before the execution of the commission and diligence; or

(b) following execution of the commission and diligence,

confidentiality may be claimed for any document produced.

(2) Where confidentiality is claimed under paragraph (1), the documents in respect of which confidentiality is claimed shall be enclosed in a separate, sealed packet.

(3) A sealed packet referred to in paragraph (2) shall not be opened except by authority of the sheriff obtained on the application of the party who sought the commission and diligence.

(4) Before the sheriff grants an application made in accordance with paragraph (3), he shall offer to hear the party or parties from whose possession the documents specified in the commission and diligence were obtained.

Witnesses

17.4.—(1) A party shall be responsible for securing the attendance of his witnesses or havers at a hearing and shall be personally liable for their expenses.

(2) The summons or the copy served on the defender shall be sufficient warrant for the citation of witnesses or havers.

(3) The citation of a witness or haver must be in Form 16 and the certificate of execution of citation must be in Form 16a.

(4) The period of notice given to witnesses or havers cited in terms of paragraph (3) must be not less than seven days.

(5) A witness or haver shall be cited—

(a) by registered post or the first class recorded delivery service by the solicitor for the party on whose behalf he is cited;

(b) by a sheriff officer—

(i) personally;

    (ii) by a citation being left with a resident at the person's dwelling place or an employee at his place of business;

    (iii) by depositing it in that person's dwelling place or place of business;

    (iv) by affixing it to the door of that person's dwelling place or place of business; or

    (v) by registered post or the first class recorded delivery service.

(6) Where service is effected under paragraph 5(b)(iii) or (iv), the sheriff officer shall, as soon as possible after such service, send by ordinary post to the address at which he thinks it most likely that the person may be found, a letter containing a copy of the citation.

Citation of witnesses by party litigants

17.5.—(1) Where a party to a claim is a party litigant he shall—

    (a) not later than 28 days before any hearing on evidence apply to the sheriff to fix caution for expenses in such sum as the sheriff considers reasonable having regard to the number of witnesses he proposes to cite and the period for which they may be required to attend court; and

    (b) before instructing a solicitor or a sheriff officer to cite a witness, find the sum fixed in accordance with paragraph (1)(a).

(2) A party litigant who does not intend to cite all the witnesses referred to in his application under paragraph (1)(a) may apply for variation of the amount of caution.

Witnesses failing to attend

17.6.—(1) A hearing must not be adjourned solely on account of the failure of a witness to appear unless the sheriff, on cause shown, so directs.

(2) A witness or haver who fails without reasonable excuse to answer a citation after having been properly cited and offered his travelling expenses if he has asked for them may be ordered by the sheriff to pay a penalty not exceeding £250.

(3) The sheriff may grant decree for payment of a penalty imposed under paragraph (2) above in favour of the party on whose behalf the witness or haver was cited.

(4) The sheriff may grant warrant for the apprehension of the witness or haver and for bringing him to court.

(5) A warrant mentioned in paragraph (4) shall be effective in any sheriffdom without endorsation and the expenses of it may be awarded against the witness or haver.

CHAPTER 18

European Court

Interpretation of rules 18.2 to 18.5

18.1.—(1) In rules 18.2 to 18.5—

"the European Court" means the Court of Justice of the European Communities;

"reference" means a reference to the European Court for—

(a) a preliminary ruling under Article 234 of the E.E.C. Treaty, Article 150 of the Euratom Treaty or Article 41 of the E.C.S.C. Treaty; or

(b) a ruling on the interpretation of the Conventions, as defined in section 1(1) of the Civil Jurisdiction and Judgments Act 1982, under Article 3 of Schedule 2 to that Act.

(2) The expressions "E.E.C. Treaty", "Euratom Treaty" and "E.C.S.C. Treaty" have the meanings assigned respectively in Schedule 1 to the European Communities Act 1972.

Application for reference

18.2.—(1) The sheriff may, on the incidental application of a party, or of his own accord, make a reference.

(2) A reference must be made in the form of a request for a preliminary ruling of the European Court in Form 17.

Preparation of case for reference

18.3.—(1) If the sheriff decides that a reference shall be made, he must within four weeks draft a reference.

(2) On the reference being drafted, the sheriff clerk must send a copy to each party.

(3) Within four weeks after the date on which copies of the draft have been sent to parties, each party may—

(a) lodge with the sheriff clerk; and

(b) send to every other party,

a note of any adjustments he seeks to have made in the draft reference.

(4) Within 14 days after the date on which any such note of adjustments may be lodged, the sheriff, after considering any such adjustments, must make and sign the reference.

(5) The sheriff clerk must forthwith intimate the making of the reference to each party.

Sist of claim

18.4.—(1) Subject to paragraph (2), on a reference being made, the claim must, unless the sheriff when making the reference otherwise orders, be sisted until the European Court has given a preliminary ruling on the question referred to it.

(2) The sheriff may recall a sist made under paragraph (1) for the purpose of making an interim order which a due regard to the interests of the parties may require.

Transmission of reference

18.5. A copy of the reference, certified by the sheriff clerk, must be transmitted by the sheriff clerk to the Registrar of the European Court.

CHAPTER 19

Abandonment

Abandonment of claim

19.1.—(1) At any time prior to decree being granted, the pursuer may offer to abandon the claim.

(2) If the pursuer offers to abandon, the sheriff clerk must assess the expenses payable by the pursuer to the defender on such basis as the sheriff may direct subject to the provisions of section 36B of the 1971 Act and rule 21.6, and the claim must be continued to the first appropriate court occurring not sooner than 14 days thereafter.

(3) If before the continued diet the pursuer makes payment to the defender of the amount fixed under paragraph (2), the sheriff must dismiss the action unless the pursuer consents to absolvitor.

(4) If before the continued diet the pursuer fails to pay the amount fixed under paragraph (2), the defender shall be entitled to decree of absolvitor with expenses.

CHAPTER 20

Decree by default

Decree by default

20.1.—(1) If, after the sheriff has fixed a hearing on evidence under rule 9.2(4), any party fails to appear or be represented at a hearing, the sheriff may grant decree by default.

(2) If all parties fail to appear or be represented at a hearing referred to at paragraph (1) the sheriff must, unless sufficient reason appears to the contrary, dismiss the claim and any counterclaim.

(3) If, after a defence has been stated, a party fails to implement an order of the court, the sheriff may, after giving him an opportunity to be heard, grant decree by default.

(4) The sheriff shall not grant decree by default solely on the grounds that a party has failed to appear at the hearing of an incidental application.

CHAPTER 21

Decrees, extracts, execution and variation

Decree

21.1.—(1) The sheriff must not grant decree against—

(a) a defender in respect of a claim; or
(b) a pursuer in respect of a counterclaim,

under any provision of these Rules unless satisfied that a ground of jurisdiction exists.

Decree for alternative claim for payment

21.2.—(1) If the sheriff has granted decree for—

(a) delivery;

(b) recovery of possession of moveable property; or

(c) implement of an obligation,

and the defender fails to comply with that decree, the pursuer may lodge with the sheriff clerk an incidental application for decree in terms of the alternative claim for payment.

(2) If the pursuer lodges an incidental application in terms of paragraph (1), he must intimate it to the defender at or before the time it is lodged with the sheriff clerk.

(3) The pursuer must appear at the hearing of an incidental application under paragraph (1).

Taxes on funds under control of the court

21.3. In a claim in which money has been consigned into court under the Sheriff Court Consignations (Scotland) Act 1893, no decree, warrant or order for payment to any person shall be granted until there has been lodged with the sheriff clerk a certificate by an authorised officer of the Inland Revenue stating that all taxes or duties payable to the Commissioners of Inland Revenue have been paid or satisfied.

Correction of interlocutor or note

21.4. At any time before extract, the sheriff may correct any clerical or incidental error in an interlocutor or note attached to it.

Extract of decree

21.5.—(1) Unless the sheriff on application authorises earlier extract, extract of a decree signed by the sheriff clerk may be issued only after the lapse of 14 days from the granting of the decree.

(2) An application for early extract shall be made by incidental application.

(3) In a claim where an appeal has been lodged, the extract may not be issued until the appeal has been disposed of.

(4) The extract decree—

(a) may be written on the summons or on a separate paper;

(b) may be in one of Forms 18 to 18ı; and

(c) shall be warrant for all lawful execution.

Expenses

21.6.—(1) This rule applies, subject to section 36B of the 1971 Act, to the determination of expenses—

(a) in a claim, where the defender has—

(i) not stated a defence;

(ii) having stated a defence, has not proceeded with it; or

(iii) having stated a defence, has not acted in good faith as to its merits; and

(b) in an appeal to the sheriff principal.

(2) Subject to paragraphs (3) to (5), the sheriff clerk must, with the approval of the sheriff, assess the amount of expenses including the fees and outlays of witnesses awarded

in any claim, in accordance with the statutory table of fees of solicitors appropriate to a summary cause.

(3) Paragraph (4) applies to a party who—

(a) represents himself;
(b) is represented by an authorised lay representative; or
(c) is not an individual and—
    (i) is represented by an authorised lay representative; and
    (ii) if unrepresented could not represent itself.

(4) A party mentioned in paragraph (3) who, if he had been represented by a solicitor or advocate would have been entitled to expenses, may be awarded any outlays or expenses to which he might be found entitled by virtue of the 1975 Act or any enactment under that Act.

(5) In every case including an appeal where expenses are awarded, the sheriff clerk shall hear the parties or their solicitors on the claims for expenses including fees, if any, and outlays.

(6) Except where the sheriff principal or the sheriff has reserved judgment or where he orders otherwise, the hearing on the claim for expenses must take place immediately upon the decision being pronounced.

(7) When that hearing is not held immediately, the sheriff clerk must—

(a) fix the date, time and place when he shall hear the parties or their solicitors; and
(b) give all parties at least 14 days' notice in writing of the hearing so fixed.

(8) The party awarded expenses must—

(a) lodge his account of expenses in court at least seven days prior to the date of any hearing fixed under paragraph (7); and
(b) at the same time forward a copy of that account to every other party.

(9) The sheriff clerk must—

(a) fix the amount of the expenses; and
(b) report his decision to the sheriff principal or the sheriff in open court for his approval at a diet which the sheriff clerk has intimated to the parties.

(10) The sheriff principal or the sheriff, after hearing parties or their solicitors if objections are stated, must pronounce final decree for payment of expenses as approved by him.

(11) In an appeal, the sheriff may pronounce decree under paragraph (10) on behalf of the sheriff principal.

(12) Failure by—

(a) any party to comply with any of the foregoing provisions of this rule; or
(b) the successful party or parties to appear at the hearing on expenses,

must be reported by the sheriff clerk to the sheriff principal or the sheriff at a diet which the sheriff clerk has intimated to the parties.

(13) In either of the circumstances mentioned in paragraphs (12)(a) or (b), the sheriff principal or sheriff must, unless sufficient cause be shown, pronounce decree on the merits of the claim and find no expenses due to or by any party.

(14) A decree pronounced under paragraph (13) shall be held to be the final decree for the purposes of these Rules.

(15) The sheriff principal or sheriff may, if he thinks fit, on the application of the solicitor of any party to whom expenses may be awarded, made at or before the time of the final decree being pronounced, grant decree in favour of that solicitor for the expenses of the claim.

Charge

21.7.—(1) The period for payment specified in any charge following on a decree for payment granted in a claim shall be—

(a) 14 days if the person on whom it is served is within the United Kingdom; and
(b) 28 days if he is outside the United Kingdom or his whereabouts are unknown.

(2) The period in respect of any other form of charge on a decree granted in a claim shall be 14 days.

Service of charge where address of defender is unknown

21.8.—(1) If the address of a defender is not known to the pursuer, a charge shall be deemed to have been served on the defender if it is—

(a) served on the sheriff clerk of the sheriff court district where the defender's last known address is located; and
(b) displayed by the sheriff clerk on the walls of court for the period of the charge.

(2) On receipt of such a charge, the sheriff clerk must display it on the walls of court and it must remain displayed for the period of the charge.
(3) The period specified in the charge shall run from the first date on which it was displayed on the walls of court.
(4) On the expiry of the period of charge, the sheriff clerk must endorse a certificate in Form 19 on the charge certifying that it has been displayed in accordance with this rule and must thereafter return the charge to the sheriff officer by whom service was executed.

Diligence on decree in claim for delivery

21.9.—(1) In a claim for delivery, the court may, when granting decree, grant warrant to search for and take possession of goods and to open shut and lockfast places.
(2) A warrant granted under paragraph (1) shall only apply to premises occupied by the defender.

Applications in same claim for variation, etc. of decree

21.10.—(1) If by virtue of any enactment the sheriff, without a new action being initiated, may order that—

(a) a decree granted be varied, discharged or rescinded; or
(b) the execution of that decree in so far as it has not already been executed be sisted or suspended,

the party requesting the sheriff to make such an order must do so by lodging a minute to that effect, setting out briefly the reasons for the application.

(2) On the lodging of such a minute by the pursuer, the sheriff clerk must grant warrant for service upon the defender (provided that the pursuer has returned the extract decree).

(3) On the lodging of such a minute by the defender, the sheriff clerk must grant warrant for service upon the pursuer ordaining him to return the extract decree and may, where appropriate, grant interim sist of execution of the decree.

(4) Subject to paragraph (5), the minute shall not be heard in court unless seven days' notice of the minute and warrant has been given to the other parties by the party lodging the minute.

(5) The sheriff may, on cause shown, alter the period of seven days referred to in paragraph (4) but may not reduce it to less than two days.

(6) This rule shall not apply to any proceedings under the Debtors (Scotland) Act 1987 or to proceedings which may be subject to the provisions of that Act.

CHAPTER 22

Recall of decree

Recall of decree
22.1.—(1) A party may apply for recall of a decree granted under rule 8.1(3), rule 9.1(6), (7) or (8) or rule 11.1(8) by lodging with the sheriff clerk a minute in Form 20, explaining the party's failure to appear and in the case of—

(a) a defender; or
(b) where decree has been granted in respect of a counterclaim, a pursuer,

stating, where he has not already done so—

(i) his proposed defence, in the case of a defender; or
(ii) his proposed answer, in the case of a pursuer responding to a counterclaim.

(2) A party may apply for recall of a decree in the same claim on one occasion only.

(3) Except in relation to an application to which paragraph (4) applies, a minute by a pursuer under paragraph (1) must be lodged within 14 days of the grant of the decree.

(4) A minute lodged by—

(a) a pursuer in respect of a decree granted in terms of a counterclaim; or
(b) a defender,

shall be lodged—

(i) if the claim has been served outwith the United Kingdom under rule 6.5, within a reasonable time after he had knowledge of the decree against him or in any event before the expiry of one year from the date of that decree; or
(ii) in any other case, within 14 days of the execution of a charge or execution of arrestment, whichever first occurs, following on the grant of decree.

(5) On the lodging of a minute for recall of a decree, the sheriff clerk must fix a date, time and place for a hearing of the minute.

(6) If a hearing has been fixed under paragraph (5), the party seeking recall must serve upon the other party not less than seven days before the date fixed for the hearing—

(a) a copy of the minute in Form 20a; and
(b) a note of the date, time and place of the hearing.

(7) If the party seeking recall—

(a) is not a partnership or body corporate;
(b) is not acting in a representative capacity; and
(c) is not represented by a solicitor,

the sheriff clerk must assist that party to complete and lodge the minute for recall and must arrange service of it—

(i) by first class recorded delivery post; or
(ii) on payment of the fee prescribed by the Scottish Ministers by order, by sheriff officer.

(8) At a hearing fixed under paragraph (5), the sheriff shall recall the decree so far as not implemented and the hearing shall then proceed as the Hearing held in terms of rule 9.1(2).

(9) A minute for recall of a decree, when lodged and served in terms of this rule, shall have the effect of preventing any further action being taken by the other party to enforce the decree.

(10) On receipt of the copy minute for recall of a decree, any party in possession of an extract decree must return it forthwith to the sheriff clerk.

(11) If it appears to the sheriff that there has been any failure or irregularity in service of the minute for recall of a decree, he may order re-service of the minute on such conditions as he thinks fit.

CHAPTER 23

Appeals

Appeals
23.1.—(1) An appeal to the sheriff principal, other than an appeal to which rule 23.4 applies, must be by note of appeal in Form 21 and lodged with the sheriff clerk not later than 14 days after the date of final decree—

(a) requesting a stated case; and
(b) specifying the point of law upon which the appeal is to proceed.

(2) The appellant must, at the same time as lodging a note of appeal, intimate a copy of it to every other party.

(3) The sheriff must, within 28 days of the lodging of a note of appeal, issue a draft stated case containing—

(a) findings in fact and law or, where appropriate, a narrative of the proceedings before him;
(b) appropriate questions of law; and

(c) a note stating the reasons for his decisions in law,

and the sheriff clerk must send a copy of the draft stated case to the parties.

(4) Within 14 days of the issue of the draft stated case—

(a) a party may lodge with the sheriff clerk a note of any adjustments which he seeks to make;

(b) a respondent may state any point of law which he wishes to raise in the appeal; and

(c) the note of adjustment and, where appropriate, point of law must be intimated to every other party.

(5) The sheriff may, on the motion of a party or of his own accord, and must where he proposes to reject any proposed adjustment, allow a hearing on adjustments and may provide for such further procedure under this rule prior to the hearing of the appeal as he thinks fit.

(6) The sheriff must, within 14 days after—

(a) the latest date on which a note of adjustments has been or may be lodged; or

(b) where there has been a hearing on adjustments, that hearing,

and after considering such note and any representations made to him at the hearing, state and sign the case.

(7) If the sheriff is temporarily absent from duty for any reason, the sheriff principal may extend any period specified in paragraphs (3) or (6) for such period or periods as he considers reasonable.

(8) The stated case signed by the sheriff must include questions of law, framed by him, arising from the points of law stated by the parties and such other questions of law as he may consider appropriate.

(9) After the sheriff has signed the stated case, the sheriff clerk must—

(a) place before the sheriff principal all documents and productions in the case together wit the stated case; and

(b) send to the parties a copy of the stated case together with a written note of the date, time and place of the hearing of the appeal.

Effect of and abandonment of appeal

23.2.—(1) When a note of appeal has been lodged, it may be insisted on by all other parties in the claim although they may not have lodged separate appeals.

(2) After a note of appeal has been lodged, the appellant shall not be at liberty to withdraw it, except—

(a) with the consent of the other parties which may be incorporated in a joint minute; or

(b) by leave of the sheriff principal and on such terms as to expenses or otherwise as to him seem proper.

Hearing of appeal

23.3.—(1) The sheriff principal shall hear the parties or their solicitors orally on all matters connected with the appeal included liability for expenses, but if any party moves that the question of liability for expenses be heard after the sheriff principal has given his decision the sheriff principal may grant that motion.

(2) In the hearing of an appeal, a party shall not be allowed to raise questions of law of which notice has not been given except on cause shown and subject to such conditions as to expenses or otherwise as the sheriff principal may consider appropriate.

(3) The sheriff principal may permit a party to amend any question of law or to add any new question in accordance with paragraph (2).

(4) The sheriff principal may—

(a) adhere to or vary the decree appealed against;
(b) recall the decree appealed against and substitute another therefor; or
(c) remit, if he considers it desirable, to the sheriff, for any reason other than to have further evidence led.

(5) At the conclusion of the hearing, the sheriff principal may either pronounce his decision or reserve judgment in which case he must give his decision in writing within 28 days and the sheriff clerk must forthwith intimate it to the parties.

Appeal in relation to a time to pay direction

23.4.—(1) This rule applies to appeals to the sheriff principal or to the Court of Session which relate solely to any application in connection with a time to pay direction.

(2) Rules 23.1, 23.2 and 23.3(2) and (3) shall not apply to appeals under this rule.

(3) An application for leave to appeal against a decision in an application for a time to pay direction or any order connected therewith must—

(a) be made in Form 22, within seven days of that decision, to the sheriff who made the decision; and
(b) must specify the question of law upon which the appeal is to proceed.

(4) If leave to appeal is granted, the appeal must be lodged in Form 23 and intimated by the appellant to every other party within 14 days of the order granting leave and the sheriff must state in writing his reasons for his original decision.

(5) An appeal under this rule to the sheriff principal shall proceed in accordance with paragraphs (1), (4) and (5) of rule 23.3.

Sheriff to regulate interim possession

23.5.—(1) Notwithstanding an appeal, the sheriff shall have power—

(a) to regulate all matters relating to interim possession;
(b) to make any order for the preservation of any property to which the claim relates or for its sale, if perishable;
(c) to make any order for the preservation of evidence; or
(d) to make in his discretion any interim order which a due regard for the interests of the parties may require.

(2) An order under paragraph (1) shall not be subject to review except by the appellate court at the hearing of the appeal.

CHAPTER 24

Management of damages payable to persons under legal disability

Orders for payment and management of money
24.1.—(1) In a claim of damages in which a sum of money becomes payable, by virtue of a decree or an extra-judicial settlement, to or for the benefit of a person under legal disability (other than a person under the age of 18 years), the sheriff shall make such order regarding the payment and management of that sum for the benefit of that person as he thinks fit.

(2) Any order required under paragraph (1) shall be made on the granting of decree for payment or of absolvitor.

Methods of management
24.2. In making an order under rule 24.1(1), the sheriff may—

(a) order the money to be paid to—
  (i) the Accountant of Court, or
  (ii) the guardian of the person under legal disability,
  as trustee, to be applied, invested or otherwise dealt with and administered under the directions of the sheriff for the benefit of the person under legal disability;
(b) order the money to be paid to the sheriff clerk of the sheriff court district in which the person under legal disability resides, to be applied, invested or otherwise dealt with and administered, under the directions of the sheriff of that district, for the benefit of the person under legal disability; or
(c) order the money to be paid directly to the person under legal disability.

Subsequent orders
24.3.—(1) If the sheriff has made an order under rule 24.1(1), any person having an interest may apply for an order under rule 24.2, or any other order for the payment or management of the money, by incidental application.

(2) An application for directions under rule 24.2(a) or (b) may be made by any person having an interest by incidental application.

Management of money paid to sheriff clerk
24.4.—(1) A receipt in Form 24 by the sheriff clerk shall be a sufficient discharge in respect of the amount paid to him under rules 24.1 to 24.3.

(2) The sheriff clerk shall, at the request of any competent court, accept custody of any sum of money in a claim of damages ordered to be paid to, applied, invested or otherwise dealt with by him, for the benefit of a person under legal disability.

(3) Any money paid to the sheriff clerk under rules 24.1 to 24.3 must be paid out, applied, invested or otherwise dealt with by the sheriff clerk only after such intimation, service and enquiry as the sheriff may order.

(4) Any sum of money invested by the sheriff clerk under rules 24.1 to 24.3 must be invested in a manner in which trustees are authorised to invest by virtue of the Trustee Investments Act 1961.

Management of money payable to children
24.5. If the sheriff has made an order under section 13 of the Children (Scotland) Act 1995, an application by a person for an order by virtue of section 11(1)(d) of that Act must be made in writing.

CHAPTER 25

Electronic transmission of documents

Extent of provision
25.1.—(1) Any document referred to in these rules which requires to be—

(a) lodged with the sheriff clerk;
(b) intimated to a party; or
(c) sent by the sheriff clerk,

may be in electronic or documentary form, and if in electronic form may be lodged, intimated or sent by e-mail or similar means.

(2) Paragraph (1) does not apply to any certificate of execution of service, citation or arrestment, or to a decree or extract decree of the court.
(3) Where any document is lodged by e-mail or similar means the sheriff may require any principal document to be lodged.

Time of lodgement
25.2. The time of lodgement, intimation or sending shall be the time when the document was sent or transmitted.

Appendix 1

Rule 1.1(4)

FORMS

Rule 4.1(1)

FORM 1

Summons

Sheriff Court (name, address, e-mail and telephone no.)	**1**	
Name and address of person making the claim (**pursuer**)	**2**	
Name and address of person against whom claim made (**defender**)	**3**	
Claim (form of decree or other order sought)	**4**	
Name, full address, telephone no, and e-mail address of pursuer's solicitor or authorised lay representative (if any) acting in the claim	**5**	
Fee Details (Enter these only if forms sent electronically to court)	**5a**	

	6	**RETURN DAY** **20**
		HEARING DATE **20** at am.

* Sheriff Clerk to delete as appropriate

The pursuer is authorised to serve a copy summons in Form *1a/1b, on the defender(s) not less than *21/42 days before the **RETURN DAY** shown in the box above. The summons is warrant for service, *arrestment on the dependence and for citation of witnesses to attend court on any future date at which evidence may be led.

Court Authentication

-

NOTE: The pursuer should complete boxes 1 to 5a, and the statement of claim on page 2. The sheriff clerk will complete box 6.

---

7.   **STATE DETAILS OF CLAIM HERE OR ATTACH A STATEMENT OF CLAIM**

     (To be completed by the pursuer. If space is insufficient, a separate sheet may be attached)

     The details of the claim are:

     FOR OFFICIAL USE ONLY

     Sheriff's notes as to:

     1.   Issues of fact and law in dispute
     2.   Facts agreed
     3.   Directions and guidance upon evidence to be led

Rule 4.3(a)

FORM 1a

*Defender's copy summons – claim for or including claim for payment of money
where time to pay direction or time order may be applied for*

**DEFENDER'S COPY: Claim for or including payment of money (where time to pay
direction or time order may be applied for)**

Sheriff Court (name, address, e-mail and telephone no.)	**1**	
Name and address of person making the claim (**pursuer**)	**2**	
Name and address of person against whom claim made (**defender**)	**3**	
Claim (form of decree or other order sought – *complete as in section 1 of Form 1*)	**4**	
Name, full address, telephone no, and e-mail address of pursuer's solicitor or authorised lay representative (if any) acting in the claim	**5**	

6	**RETURN DAY**	**20**		
	HEARING DATE	**20**	**at**	**am.**

NOTE: You will find details of claim on page 2.

7.   STATE DETAILS OF CLAIM HERE OR ATTACH A STATEMENT OF
      CLAIM
      (To be completed by the pursuer. If space is insufficient, a separate sheet
      may be attached)

      The details of the claim are:

8.   SERVICE ON DEFENDER

              (Place)   (Date)

              To: (defender)

      You are hereby served with a copy of the above summons.

                                        Solicitor/sheriff officer
                                        delete as appropriate

NOTE: The pursuer should complete boxes 1 to 6 on page 1, the statement of
claim in box 7 on page 2 and section A on page 5 before service on the defender.
The person serving the summons will complete box 8.

WHAT MUST I DO ABOUT THIS SUMMONS?

Decide whether you wish to dispute the claim and/or whether you owe any money or not, and how you wish to proceed. Then, look at the 4 options listed below. Find the one which covers your decision and follow the instructions given there. You will find the RETURN DAY and the HEARING DATE on page one of the summons.

Written guidance on small claims procedure can be obtained from the sheriff clerk at any sheriff clerk's office. Further advice can also be obtained by contacting any of the following:

> **Citizen's Advice Bureau, Consumer Advice Centre, Trading Standards or Consumer Protection Department or a Solicitor. (Addresses can be found in the guidance booklets.)**

OPTIONS

1.   **ADMIT LIABILITY FOR THE CLAIM and settle it with the pursuer now.**

   If you wish to avoid the possibility of a court order passing against you, you should settle the claim (including any question of expenses) with pursuer or his representative **in good time before the return day.** Please do not send any payment direct to the court. Any payment should be made to the pursuer or his representative.

2.   **ADMIT LIABILITY FOR THE CLAIM and make a written application to pay by instalments or by deferred lump sum.**

   Complete box 1 of section B on page 5 of this form and return pages 5 and 6 to the court **to arrive on or before the return day.** You should then contact the court to find out whether or not the pursuer has accepted your offer. If he has not accepted it, the case will then call on the hearing date and the court will decide how the amount claimed is to be paid.

   If the claim is for delivery, or implement of an obligation, and you wish to pay the alternative amount claimed, you may also wish to make an application about the method of payment. If so, follow the instructions in the previous paragraph.

   NOTE: If you fail to return pages 5 and 6 as directed, or if, having returned them, you fail to attend or are not represented at the hearing date if the case is to call, the court will almost certainly decide the claim in your absence.

3.   **ADMIT LIABILITY FOR THE CLAIM and attend at court to make application to pay by instalments or deferred lump sum.**

   Complete box 2 on page 5. Return page 5 to the court so that it arrives **on or before the return day.**

If the claim is for delivery, or implement of an obligation, you may wish to pay the alternative amount claimed, and attend at court to make an application about the method of payment.

You must attend personally, or be represented, at court on the hearing date. Your representative may be a solicitor, or someone else having your authority. It may be helpful if you or your representative bring pages 1 and 2 of this form to the court.

NOTE: If you fail to return page 5 as directed, or if, having returned it, you fail to attend or are not represented on the hearing date, the court will almost certainly decide the claim in your absence.

4.   **DISPUTE THE CLAIM and <u>attend at court</u> to do any of the following:**

*   Challenge the jurisdiction of the court
*   State a defence
*   State a counterclaim
*   Dispute the amount of the claim

Complete box 3 on page 5. Return page 5 to the court so that it arrives **on or before the return day. You must attend personally, or be represented, at court on the hearing date.**

Your representative may be a solicitor, or someone else having your authority. It may be helpful if you or your representative bring pages 1 and 2 of this form to the court.

NOTE: If you fail to return page 5 as directed, or if, having returned it, you fail to attend or are not represented on the hearing date, the court will almost certainly decide the claim in your absence.

WRITTEN NOTE OR PROPOSED COUNTERCLAIM

You may send to the court a written note of any counterclaim. If you do, you should also send a copy to the pursuer. You must also attend or be represented at court on the hearing date.

PLEASE NOTE

If you do nothing about this summons, the court will almost certainly, where appropriate, grant decree against you and order you to pay to the pursuer the sum claimed, including any interest and expenses found due.

If the summons is for delivery, or implement of an obligation, the court may order your to deliver the article or perform the duty in question within a specified period. If you fail to do so, the court may order you to pay to the pursuer the alternative amount claimed, including interest and expenses.

YOU ARE ADVISED TO KEEP PAGES 1 AND 2, AS THEY MAY BE USEFUL AT A LATER STAGE OF THE CASE.

SECTION A

This section must
be completed
before service

SHERIFF COURT (Including address)

| Summons No |
| Return Day |
| Hearing Date |

PURSUER'S FULL NAME AND ADDRESS

DEFENDER'S FULL NAME AND
ADDRESS

SECTION B   **DEFENDER'S RESPONSE TO THE SUMMONS**
                    ** Delete whichever boxes do <u>not</u> apply

**Box 1

ADMIT LIABILITY FOR THE CLAIM and make <u>written</u> application to pay by instalments or by <u>deferred</u> lump sum.

I do not intend to defend the case but admit liability for the claim and wish to pay the sum of money claimed.

I wish to make a written application about payment.

I have completed the application form on page 6.

**Box 2

ADMIT LIABILITY FOR THE CLAIM and attend at court.

I admit liability for the claim.

I wish to make application to pay the sum claimed by instalments or by deferred lump sum.

I intend to appear or be represented at court.

**Box 3

DISPUTE THE CLAIM (or the amount due) and attend at court
* I wish to dispute the amount due only.
* I intend to challenge the jurisdiction of the court.
* I intend to state a defence.
* I intend to state a counterclaim.

I intend to appear or be represented in court.

* I attach a note of my proposed counterclaim which has been copied to the pursuer.

delete as necessary

NOTE: **Please remember to send your response to the court to arrive on or before the return day if you have completed any of the responses above.**

APPLICATION IN WRITING FOR A TIME TO PAY DIRECTION
OR A TIME ORDER

I WISH TO APPLY FOR A *TIME TO PAY DIRECTION/TIME ORDER
* delete whichever does not apply

I admit the claim and make application to pay as follows:

    (1)   by instalments of £ _____ per *week / fortnight / month

        OR

    (2)   In one payment within _____ *weeks / months from the date of the court order

To help the court, please provide details of your financial position in the boxes below
*Please also indicate whether payments/receipts are weekly, fortnightly or monthly

My outgoings are:	*Weekly / fortnightly / monthly		My income is:	*Weekly / fortnightly / monthly
Rent/Mortgage	£		Wages/Pensions	£
Council tax	£		Social Security	£
Gas/electricity etc	£		Other	
Food	£			
Loans and credit agreements	£			
Other				
	TOTAL			**TOTAL**

Number of dependent children – [   ]   Number of dependent relatives [   ]

Please list details of all capital held, e.g. value of house; amount in savings account, shares or other investments:

---

*APPLICATION FOR RECALL OR RESTRICTION OF AN ARRESTMENT

I seek the recall or restriction of the arrestment of which the details are as follows:-

Date:
*Delete if inapplicable

NOTES: APPLICATION FOR A TIME TO PAY
DIRECTION OR TIME ORDER

(1) Time to pay directions

The Debtors (Scotland) Act 1987 gives you the right to apply to the court for a 'time to pay direction'. This is an order which allows you to pay any sum which the court orders you to pay either in instalments or by deferred lump sum. A 'deferred lump sum' means that you will be ordered by the court to pay the whole amount at one time within a period which the court will specify.

If the court makes a time to pay direction it may also recall or restrict any arrrestment made on your property by the pursuer in connection with the action or debt (for example, your bank account may have been frozen).

No court fee is payable when making an application for a time to pay direction.

If a time to pay direction is made, a copy of the court order (called an extract decree) will be sent to you by the pursuer telling you when payment should start or when it is you have to pay the lump sum.

If a time to pay direction is not made, and an order for immediate payment is made against you, an order to pay (called a charge) may be served on you if you do not pay.

(2) Time Orders

The Consumer Credit Act 1974 allows you to apply to the court for a 'time order' during a court action. A time order is similar to a time to pay direction, but can only be applied for in certain circumstances, e.g., in relation to certain types of credit agreement. Payment under a time order can only be made by instalments, so that you cannot apply to pay by deferred lump sum.

FORM 1b

Defender's copy summons – all other claims

DEFENDER'S COPY: Claim other than claim for or including payment of money where time to pay direction or time order may be applied for)

Sheriff Court (name, address, e-mail and telephone no.)	**1**	
Name and address of person making the claim (**pursuer**)	**2**	
Name and address of person against whom claim made (**defender**)	**3**	
Claim (Form of decree or other order sought - *complete as in section 4 of Form 1*)	**4**	
Name, full address, telephone no, and e-mail address of pursuer's solicitor or authorised lay representative (if any)	**5**	

6	**RETURN DAY**	**20**		
	HEARING DATE	**20**	at	am.

NOTE: You will find details of claim on page 2.

7.   STATE DETAILS OF CLAIM HERE OR ATTACH A STATEMENT OF CLAIM
(To be completed by the pursuer. If space is insufficient, a separate sheet may be attached)

The details of the claim are:

8.   SERVICE ON DEFENDER

(Place)   (Date)

To: (defender)

You are hereby served with a copy of the above summons.

Solicitor/sheriff officer
delete as appropriate

The pursuer should complete boxes 1 to 6 on page 1, the statement of claim in box 7 on page 2 and section A on page 4 before service on the defender. The person serving the summons will complete box 8.

WHAT MUST I DO ABOUT THIS SUMMONS?

Decide whether you wish to dispute the claim and/or whether you owe any money or not, and how you wish to proceed. Then, look at the 2 options listed below. Find the one which covers your decision and follow the instructions given there. You will find the RETURN DAY and the HEARING DATE on page one of the summons.

Written guidance on small claims procedure can be obtained from the sheriff clerk at any Sheriff Clerk's office.

Further advice can also be obtained by contacting any of the following:

Citizen's Advice Bureau, Consumer Advice Centre, Trading Standards or Consumer Protection Department or a solicitor. (Addresses can be found in the guidance booklets.)

OPTIONS

1.   **ADMIT LIABILITY FOR THE CLAIM** and settle it with the pursuer now.

If you wish to avoid the possibility of a court order passing against you, you should settle the claim (including any question of expenses) with pursuer or his representative **in good time before the return day.** Please do not send any payment direct to the court. Any payment should be made to the pursuer or his representative.

2.   **DISPUTE THE CLAIM and attend at court to do any of the following:**

* Challenge the jurisdiction of the court
* State a defence
* State a counterclaim
* Dispute the amount of the claim

Complete Section B on page 4. Return page 4 to the court so that it arrives **on or before the return day. You must attend personally, or be represented, at court on the hearing date.**

Your representative may be a solicitor, or someone else having your authority. It may be helpful if you or your representative bring pages 1 and 2 of this form to the court.

NOTE: If you fail to return page 4 as directed, or if, having returned it, you fail to attend or are not represented on the hearing date, the court will almost certainly decide the claim in your absence.

WRITTEN NOTE OF PROPOSED COUNTERCLAIM

You may send to the court a written note of any counterclaim. If you do, you should also send a copy to the pursuer. You must also attend or be represented at court on the hearing date.

PLEASE NOTE

If you do nothing about this summons, the court will almost certainly, where appropriate, grant decree against you and order you to pay to the pursuer the sum claimed, including any interest and expenses found due.

If the summons is for delivery, or implement of an obligation, the court may order you to deliver the article or perform the duty in question within a specified period. If you fail to do so, the court may order you to pay to the pursuer the alternative amount claimed, including interest and expenses.

YOU ARE ADVISED TO KEEP PAGES 1 AND 2, AS THEY MAY BE USEFUL AT A LATER STAGE OF THE CASE.

SECTION A

This section must
be completed
before service

| Summons No |
| Return Day |
| Hearing Date |

SHERIFF COURT (Including address)

PURSUER'S FULL NAME AND ADDRESS   DEFENDER'S FULL NAME AND ADDRESS

SECTION B   **DEFENDER'S RESPONSE TO THE SUMMONS**

> **DISPUTE THE CLAIM (or the amount due) and attend at court**
> * I wish to dispute the amount due only.
> * I intend to challenge the jurisdiction of the court.
> * I intend to state a defence.
> * I intend to state a counterclaim.
>
> I intend to appear or be represented in court.
>
> * I attach a note of my proposed counterclaim which has been copied to the pursuer.
>
>   *delete as necessary*

PLEASE REMEMBER: You must send this page to the court **to arrive on or before the return day** if you have completed Section B above.

If you have admitted the claim, please do not send any payment direct to the court. Any payment should be made to the pursuer or his solicitor.

FORM 2

Rule 4.1(2)

Form of claim in a summons for payment of money

The pursuer claims from the defendant(s) the sum of £ with interest on that sum at the rate of % annually from the date of service, together with the expenses of bringing the claim.

FORM 3

Rule 4.1(2)

Form of claim in a summons for delivery

The pursuer claims that, in the circumstances described in the statement contained on page 2 of this copy summons, he has right to the possession of the article(s) described therein.
He therefore asks the court to grant a decree ordering you to deliver the said articles to the pursuer.
Alternatively, if you do not deliver said articles, the pursuer asks the court to grant a decree ordering you to pay to him the sum of £ with interest on that sum at the rate of % annually from until payment.
The pursuer also claims from you the expenses of bringing the claim.

FORM 4

Rule 4.1(2)

Form of claim in a summons for implement of an obligation

The pursuer claims that, in the circumstances described in the statement contained on page 2 of the summons, you are obliged to .
He therefore asks the court to grant a decree ordering you to implement the said obligation.
Alternatively, if you do not fulfil the obligation, the pursuer asks the court to grant a decree ordering you to pay to him the sum of £ with interest on that sum at the rate of % annually from until payment.
The pursuer also claims from you the expenses of bringing the claim.

FORM 5

Rule 6.2(1)

Form of service

XY, you are hereby served with a copy of the above (or attached) summons.
(*signature of solicitor or sheriff officer*)

FORM 6

Rule 6.2(2)

Form of certificate of execution of service

(*place and date*)
I, , hereby certify that on the date of 20 , I duly cited XY to answer the foregoing summons. This I did by (*set forth of the mode of service*)
(*signature of solicitor or sheriff officer*)

FORM 7

Rule 6.3(2)

Postal service—form of notice

This letter contains a citation to or intimation from the sheriff court at . . . .
If delivery cannot be made the letter must be returned immediately to the sheriff clerk at (*insert full address*).

FORM 8

Rule 6.6(1)(a)

Service on person whose address is unknown—form of advertisement

A small claim has been raised in the sheriff court at , by AB., pursuer, against CD, defender, whose last known address was .
If the said CD wishes to defend the claim he should immediately contact the sheriff clerk's office at the above court, from whom the defender's copy summons may be obtained.

> Address of court:
> Telephone no:
> Fax no:
> E mail address:

FORM 9

Rule 6.6(1)(b)

Service on person whose address is unknown
Form of notice to be displayed on the walls of court

A small claim has been raised in this court by AB, pursuer against CD, defender, whose last known address was . . . .
If the said CD wishes to defend the claim he should immediately contact the sheriff clerk's office, from whom the defender's copy summons may be obtained.

(*date*) Displayed on the walls of court of this date.
Sheriff clerk depute.

FORM 10

Rule 7.3(4)(a)

Recall or restriction of arrestment
Certificate authorising the release of arrested funds or property

Sheriff court at (*place*)
Court ref. no.:
AB (pursuer) against CD (defender)
I, (*name*), hereby certify that the sheriff on (*date*) authorised the release of the funds or property arrested on the *dependence of the action/counterclaim to the following extent:
(*details of sheriff's order*)
(*date*) Sheriff clerk depute
* *delete as appropriate*
Copy to:
    Party instructing arrestment
    Party possessing arrested funds/property

FORM 11

Rule 8.1(2)

Form of minute—no form of response lodged by defender

Sheriff court at (*place*)
Hearing date:
In respect that the defender(s) has/have failed to lodge a form of response to the summons, the pursuer requests the court to make the orders specified in the following case(s):
Court ref. no.: Name(s) of defender(s) Minute(s)

FORM 12

Rule 8.2(2)

Form of minute—pursuer not objecting to application for a time to pay direction or time order

Sheriff court at (*place*)
Court ref. no.:
Name(s) of defender(s)
Hearing date:
I do not object to the defender's application for
    *a time to pay direction

*recall or restriction of an arrestment
*a time order
*delete as appropriate

FORM 13

Rule 8.2(4)

Form of minute—pursuer opposing an application for a time to pay direction or time order

Sheriff court at (*place*)
Court ref. no.:
Name(s) of defender(s)
Hearing date:
I oppose the defender's application for
    *a time to pay direction
    *recall or restriction of an arrestment
    *a time order
*delete as appropriate

FORM 14

Rule 11.1(8)

Counterclaim—form of intimation by sheriff clerk where pursuer fails to appear

Court ref. no.:
(AB) (*insert address*), pursuer
against
(CD) (*insert address*), defender
When the above case called in court on (*insert date*), the defender appeared (or was represented) and stated a counterclaim to the claim made by you against him.
The court continued the case until (*date*) at (*time*).
Please note that, if you fail to appear or be represented at the continued diet, the court may grant decree against you in terms of the counterclaim.
(*date*) Sheriff clerk depute

FORM 15

Rule 17.2(1)

Order by the court and certificate in optional procedure for recovery of documents

Sheriff court at (*place*)
In the claim (*court ref. no.*)
in which
AB (*design*) is the pursuer

and

CD (*design*) is the defender

To: (*name and designation of party or haver from whom the documents are sought to be recovered*).

You are hereby required to produce to the sheriff clerk at (address) within days of the service upon you of this order:

1. This order itself (which must be produced intact);

2. The certificate marked "B" attached;

3. All documents within your possession covered by the specification which is enclosed; and

4. A list of those documents.

You can produce the items listed above either:

(a) by delivering them to the sheriff clerk at the address shown above; or

(b) sending them to the sheriff clerk by registered or recorded delivery post.

(date) (*signature, name, address and designation of person serving order*)

PLEASE NOTE:

If you claim confidentiality for any of the documents produced by you, you must still produce them. However, they may be placed in a separate envelope by themselves, marked "confidential". The court will, if necessary, decide whether the envelope should be opened or not.

CERTIFICATE

B

Sheriff Court at (*place*)

In the claim (*court ref. no.*)

in which

AB (*design*) is the pursuer

and

CD (*design*) is the defender

Order for recovery of documents dated (*insert date*).

With reference to the above order and relative specification of documents, I hereby certify:

*that the documents produced herewith and the list signed by me which accompanies them are all the documents in my possession which fall under the specification.

*I have no documents in my possession falling under the specification.

*I believe that there are other documents falling within the specification which are not in my possession. These documents are (list the documents as described in the specification). These documents were last seen by me on (date) in the possession of (name and address of person/company, if known).

*I know of no documents falling within the specification which are in the possession of any other person.

*delete as appropriate

(*name*) (*date*)

FORM 16

Rule 17.4(3)

Form of witness citation

Sheriffdom of (*insert name of sheriffdom*)
at (*insert place of sheriff court*)
to AB (*design*)
You are required to attend at (*full name and address of court*) on (*day*) at (*time*) as a witness for the (*party*) in the action at the instance of CD (*design*) against EF (*design*) (*and required to bring with you*).
If you fail to attend, warrant may be granted for your arrest.
(*date*) (*signature of solicitor or sheriff officer*)
    Name of person/firm serving citation
    Address
    Telephone no.
    Fax no.
    E mail address
NOTE: Within certain specified limits **claims** for necessary outlays and loss of earnings incurred by your attendance at court as a witness will be met. **Claims** should be made to the person who has cited you to attend court. Proof of any expenses incurred may be requested and should be given to that person.
If you wish your travelling expenses to be paid prior to your attendance, you should apply for payment to the person who has cited you.
If you fail to attend without reasonable cause, having requested and been paid your travelling expenses, you may be ordered to pay a penalty not exceeding £250.

FORM 16a

Rule 17.4(3)

Form of certificate of execution of witness citation

I certify that on (*date*) I duly cited AB (*design*) to attend at (*name of court*) on (*date*) at (*time*) as a witness for the (*design party*) in the action at the instance of CD (*design*) against EF (*design*) (*and I required him to bring with him*). This I did by .
(*signature of solicitor or sheriff officer*)

FORM 17

Rule 18.2(2)

Form of reference to the European Court

REQUEST
for
PRELIMINARY RULING
of
THE COURT OF JUSTICE OF THE EUROPEAN COMMUNITIES
from

THE SHERIFFDOM OF (*insert name of sheriffdom*) at (*insert place of court*) in the cause
AB (*insert designation and address*), pursuer
against
CD (*insert designation and address*), defender
(*Here set out a clear and succinct statement of the case giving rise to the request for a ruling of the European Court in order to enable the European Court to consider and understand the issues of Community law raised and to enable governments of Member states and other interested parties to submit observations. The statement of the case should include:*

(a) *particulars of the parties;*
(b) *the history of the dispute between the parties;*
(c) *the history of the proceedings;*
(d) *the relevant facts as agreed by the parties or found by the court or, failing such agreement or finding, the contentions of the parties on such facts;*
(e) *the nature of the issues of law and fact between the parties;*
(f) *the Scots law, so far as relevant;*
(g) *the Treaty provisions or other acts, instruments or rules of Community law concerned;*
(h) *an explanation of why the reference is being made).*

The preliminary ruling of the Court of Justice of the European Communities is accordingly requested on the following questions:
1,2,etc. (*Here set out the question(s) on which the ruling is sought, identifying the Treaty provisions or other acts, instruments or rules of Community law concerned.*)
Dated the day of 20

FORM 18

Rule 21.5(4)(b)

Form of extract decree (basic)

Sheriff court Court ref. no.:
Date of decree *in absence
Pursuer(s) Defender(s)
The sheriff
and granted decree against the for payment of expenses of £ against the (*name of party*).
This extract is warrant for all lawful execution thereon.
Date Sheriff clerk depute.
**delete as appropriate*

FORM 18a

Rule 21.5(4)(b)

Form of extract decree for payment

Sheriff court Court ref. no.:
Date of decree *in absence

Pursuer(s) Defender(s)
The sheriff granted decree against the for payment to the of the undernoted sums:
(1) Sum(s) decerned for £
(2) Interest at per cent per year from (*date*) until payment.
(3) Expenses of £ against the (*name of party*).
*A time to pay direction was made under section 1(1) of the Debtors (Scotland) Act 1987.
*A time order was made under section 129(1) of the Consumer Credit Act 1974.
*The amount is payable by instalments of £ per commencing within *days/weeks/months of intimation of this extract decree.
*The amount is payable by lump sum within *days/weeks/months of intimation of this extract decree.
This extract is warrant for all lawful execution thereon.
Date Sheriff clerk depute
*delete as appropriate

FORM 18b

Rule 21.5(4)(b)

Form of extract decree in an action of delivery

Sheriff court Court ref. no.:
Date of decree *in absence
Pursuer(s)
Defender(s)
The sheriff granted decree against the defender
(1) for delivery to the pursuer of (*specify articles*)
(2) for expenses of £
*Further, the sheriff granted warrant to officers of court to (1) open shut and lockfast places occupied by the defender and (2) search for and take possession of said goods in the possession of the defender.
*delete as appropriate
This extract is warrant for all lawful execution thereon.
Date Sheriff clerk depute

FORM 18c

Rule 21.5(4)(b)

Form of extract decree in an action of delivery—payment failing delivery

Sheriff court Court ref. no.:
Date of decree *in absence
Pursuer(s)
Defender(s)
The sheriff, in respect that the defender has failed to make delivery in accordance with the decree granted in this court on (*date*), granted decree for payment against the defender of the undernoted sums:
(1) Sum(s) decerned for: £ , being the alternative amount claimed.

(2) Interest at per cent per year from (*date*) until payment.

(3) Expenses of £ against the (*name of party*).

*A time to pay direction was made under section 1(1) of the Debtors (Scotland) Act 1987.

*The amount is payable by instalments of £ per commencing within *days/weeks/months of intimation of this extract decree.

*The amount is payable by lump sum within *days/weeks/months of intimation of this extract decree.

**delete as appropriate*

This extract is warrant for all lawful execution thereon.

Date Sheriff clerk depute

FORM 18d

Rule 21.5(4)(b)

Form of extract decree
Recovery of possession of moveable property

Sheriff court Court ref. no.:

Date of decree *in absence

Pursuer(s) Defender(s)

The sheriff granted decree against the defender:

(1) Finding the pursuer entitled to recovery of possession of the article(s) (*specify*)

(2) for expenses of £

*Further, the sheriff granted warrant to officers of court to (1) open shut and lockfast places occupied by the defender and (2) search for and take possession of said goods in the possession of the defender.

**delete as appropriate*

This extract is warrant for all lawful execution thereon.

Date Sheriff clerk depute

FORM 18e

Rule 21.5(4)(b)

Form of extract decree
Recovery of possession of moveable property—payment failing recovery

Sheriff court Court ref. no.:

Date of decree *in absence

Pursuer(s) Defender(s)

The sheriff, in respect that the defender has failed to recover possession in accordance with the decree granted in this court on (*date*), granted decree for payment against the defender of the undernoted sums:

Sum(s) decerned for: £ , being the alternative amount claimed.

Interest at per cent per year from (*date*) until payment.

Expenses of £ against the (*name of party*).

*A time to pay direction was made under section 1(1) of the Debtors (Scotland) Act 1987.

**The amount is payable by instalments of £ per commencing within *days/weeks/months of intimation of this extract decree.

*The amount is payable by lump sum within *days/weeks/months of intimation of this extract decree.

*delete as appropriate

This extract is warrant for all lawful execution thereon.

Date Sheriff clerk depute

FORM 18f

Rule 21.5(4)(b)

Form of extract decree ad factum praestandum

Sheriff court Court ref. no.:

Date of decree *in absence

Pursuer(s)

Defender(s)

The sheriff

(1) ordained the defender(s)..........

(2) granted decree for payment of expenses of £ against the defender(s).

This extract is warrant for all lawful execution thereon.

Date Sheriff clerk depute

FORM 18g

Rule 21.5(4)(b)

Form of extract decree ad factum praestandum—payment upon failure to implement obligation

Sheriff court Court ref. no.:

Date of decree *in absence

Pursuer(s)

Defender(s)

The sheriff, in respect that the defender has failed to implement the obligation contained in and in accordance with the decree granted in this court on (*date*), granted decree for payment against the defender of the undernoted sums:

(1) Sum(s) decerned for: £ , being the alternative amount claimed.

(2) Interest at per cent per year from (*date*) until payment.

(3) Expenses of £ against the (*name of party*).

*A time to pay direction was made under section 1(1) of the Debtors (Scotland) Act 1987.

*The amount is payable by instalments of £ per commencing within *days/weeks/months of intimation of this extract decree.

*The amount is payable by lump sum within *days/weeks/months of intimation of this extract decree.

*delete as appropriate

This extract is warrant for all lawful execution thereon.

Date Sheriff clerk depute

FORM 18h

Rule 21.5(4)(b)

Form of extract decree of absolvitor

Sheriff court Court ref. no.:
Date of decree *in absence
Pursuer(s)
Defender(s)
The sheriff
(1) absolved the defender(s).
(2) granted decree for payment of expenses of £ against the .
The extract is warrant for all lawful execution thereon.
Date Sheriff clerk depute

FORM 18i

Rule 21.5(4)(b)

Form of extract decree of dismissal

Sheriff court Court ref. no.:
Date of decree *in absence
Pursuer(s)
Defender(s)
The sheriff
(1) dismissed the action against the defender(s).
(2) granted decree for payment of expenses of £ against the .
This extract is warrant for all lawful execution thereon.
Date Sheriff clerk depute.

FORM 19

Rule 21.8(4)

Form of certificate by sheriff clerk
Service of charge where address of defender is unknown

I certify that the foregoing charge was displayed on the walls of court on (*date*) and that
it remained so displayed for a period of (*period of charge*) from that date.
(*date*) Sheriff clerk depute

FORM 20

Rule 22.1(1)

Minute for recall of decree

Sheriff court: (*place*)
Court ref. no.:
AB (*pursuer*) against CD (*defender(s)*)
The *(*pursuer/defender*) moves the court to recall the decree pronounced on (*date*) in this case * and in which execution of a charge/arrestment was effected on (*date*).
Reason for failure to appear or be represented:
Proposed defence/answer:
Date
delete as appropriate

FORM 20a

Rule 22.1(6)

Minute for recall of decree—service copy

Sheriff court: (*place*)
Court ref. no.:
AB (*pursuer*) against CD (*defender(s)*)
The *(*pursuer/defender*) moves the court to recall the decree pronounced on (*date*) in this case * and in which execution of a charge/arrestment was effected on (*date*).
Reason for failure to appear or be represented:
Proposed defence/answer:
Date
delete as appropriate
NOTE: You must return the summons to the sheriff clerk at the court mentioned at the top of this form by (insert date 2 days before the date of the hearing).

FORM 21

Rule 23.1(1)

Form of note of appeal to the sheriff principal

Sheriff court (*place*)
Court ref. no.:
AB (*pursuer*) against CD (*defender(s)*)
The pursuer/defender appeals the sheriff's interlocutor of (*date*) to the sheriff principal and requests the sheriff to state a case.
The point(s) of law upon which the appeal is to proceed is/are: (*give brief statement*).
(*date*)

FORM 22

Rule 23.4(3)(a)

Application for leave to appeal against time to pay direction

Sheriff court (*place*)
Court ref. no.:
AB (*pursuer*) against CD (*defender(s)*)
The pursuer/defender requests the sheriff to grant leave to appeal the decision made on (*date*) in respect of the defender's application for a time to pay direction to the sheriff principal/Court of Session.
The point(s) of law upon which the appeal is to proceed is/are: (*give brief statement*).
(*date*)

FORM 23

Rule 23.4(4)

Appeal against time to pay direction

Sheriff court (*place*)
Court ref. no.:
AB (*pursuer*) against CD (*defender(s)*)
The pursuer/defender appeals the decision made on (*date*) in respect of the defender's application for a time to pay direction to the sheriff principal/Court of Session.
(*date*)

FORM 24

Rule 24.4(1)

Form of receipt for money paid to sheriff clerk

In the sheriff court of (*name of sheriffdom*) at (*place of sheriff court*).
In the claim (*state names of parties or other appropriate description*)
AB (designation) has this day paid into court the sum of £ , being a payment made in terms of Chapter 24 of the Small Claim Rules 2002.
*Custody of this money has been accepted at the request of (*insert name of court making the request*).
*delete as appropriate
(Date) Sheriff clerk depute

Appendix 2

GLOSSARY

Absolve
To find in favour of and exonerate the defender.

Absolvitor
An order of the court granted in favour of and exonerating the defender which means that the pursuer is not allowed to bring the same matter to court again.

Appellant
A person making an appeal against the sheriff's decision. This might be the pursuer or the defender.

Arrestee
A person subject to an arrestment.

Arrestment on the dependence
A court order to freeze the goods or bank account of the defender until the court has heard the case.

Arrestment to found jurisdiction
A court order used against a person who has goods or other assets in Scotland to give the court jurisdiction to hear a claim. This is achieved by preventing anything being done with the goods or assets until the case has been disposed of.

Authorised lay representative
A person other than a lawyer who represents a party to a small claim.

Cause
Another word for case or claim, used for cases under the summary cause procedure.

Caution (pronounced *kay-shun*)
A security, usually a sum of money, given to ensure that some obligation will be carried out.

Certificate of execution of service
The document recording that an application to, or order or decree of, the court for service of documents has been effected.

Charge
An order to obey a decree of a court. A common type is one served on the defender by a sheriff officer on behalf of the pursuer who has won a case demanding payment of a sum of money.

Commission and diligence
Authorisation by the court for someone to take the evidence of a witness who cannot attend court or to obtain the production of documentary evidence. It is combined with a diligence authorising the person appointed to require the attendance of the witness and the disclosure of documents.

Consignation
The deposit in court, or with a third party, of money or an article in dispute.

Continuation
An order made by the sheriff postponing the completion of a hearing until a later date or dates.

Counterclaim
A claim made by a defender in response to the pursuer's claim and which is not a defence to that claim. It is a separate but related claim against the pursuer which is dealt with at the same time as the pursuer's claim.

Damages
Money compensation payable for a breach of contract or some other legal duty.

Decree
An order of the court containing the decision of the claim in favour of one of the parties and granting the remedy sought or disposing of the claim.

Defender
Person against whom a claim is made.

Deliverance
A decision or order of a court.

Depending
A case is said to be depending when it is going through a court procedure. Technically, this begins with citation of the defender and ends with any final appeal.

Diet
Date for a court hearing.

Diligence
The collective term for the procedures used to enforce a decree of a court. These include arrestment of wages, goods or a bank account.

Dismissal
An order bringing to an end the proceedings in a claim. It is usually possible for a new claim to be brought if not time barred.

Domicile
The place where a person is normally resident or where, in the case of a company, it has its place of business or registered office.

Execution of service
See Certificate of execution of service.

Execution of a charge
The intimation of the requirement to obey a decree or order of a court.

Execution of an arrestment
The carrying out of an order of arrestment.

Expenses
The costs of a court case.

Extra-judicial settlement
An agreement between the parties to a case to settle it themselves rather than to await a decision by the sheriff.

Extract decree
The document containing the order of the court made at the end of the claim. For example, it can be used to enforce payment of a sum awarded.

Haver
A person who holds documents which are required as evidence in a case.

Huissier
An official in France and some other European countries who serves court documents.

Incidental application
An application that can be made during the course of a small claim for certain orders. Examples are applications for the recovery of documents or to amend the statement of claim.

Interlocutor
The official record of the order or judgment of a court.

Intimation
Giving notice to another party of some step in the small claim.

Jurisdiction
The authority of a court to hear particular cases.

Messenger at arms
Officers of court who serve documents issued by the Court of Session.

Minute
A document produced in the course of a case in which a party makes an application or sets out his position on some matter.

Minute for recall
A form lodged with the court by one party asking the court to recall a decree.

Options Hearing
A preliminary stage in an ordinary cause action.

Ordinary cause
Another legal procedure for higher value claims available in the sheriff court.

Party litigant
A person who conducts his own case.

Productions
Documents or articles which are used in evidence.

Pursuer
The person making a claim.

Recall of an arrestment
A court order withdrawing an arrestment.

Restriction of an arrestment
An order releasing part of the money or property arrested.

Recall of a decree
An order revoking a decree which has been granted.

Recovery of documents
The process of obtaining documentary evidence which is not in the possession of the person seeking it (e.g. hospital records necessary to establish the extent of injuries received in a road accident).

Remit between procedures
A decision of the sheriff to transfer the claim to another court procedure e.g. summary cause or ordinary cause procedure.

Respondent
When a decision of the sheriff is appealed against, the person making the appeal is called the appellant. The other side in the appeal is called the respondent.

Return day
The date by which the defender must send a written reply to the court and, where appropriate, the pursuer must return the summons to court.

Schedule of arrestment
The list of items which may be arrested.

Service/Service
Sending a copy of the summons or other court document to the defender or another party.

Sheriff clerk
The court official responsible for the administration of the sheriff court.

Sheriff officer
A person who serves court documents and enforces court orders.

Sist of action
The temporary suspension of a court case by court order.

Sist as a party
To add another person as a litigant in a case.

Stated case
An appeal procedure where the sheriff sets out his findings and the reasons for his decision and states the issues on which the decision of the sheriff principal is requested.

Statement of claim
The part of the summons in which pursuers set out details of their claims against defenders.

Summary cause
Another legal procedure available in the Sheriff Court. It is used for certain types of claim usually having a higher value than small claims though less than those dealt with as ordinary causes.

Summons
The form which must be filled in to begin a small claim.

Time to pay direction
A court order for which a defender who is an individual may apply permitting a sum owed to be paid by instalments or by a single payment at a later date.

Time order
A court order which assists debtors who have defaulted on an agreement regulated by the Consumer Credit Act 1974 (c.39) and which may be applied for during a court action.

Warrant for diligence
Authority to carry out one of the diligence procedures.

Writ
A legally significant writing.

SCHEDULE 2

Paragraph 4

REVOCATIONS

(1)	(2)	(3)
Act of Sederunt	*Reference*	*Extent of revocation*
Act of Sederunt (Small Claim Rules) 1988	S.I. 1988/1976	The whole Act of Sederunt
Act of Sederunt (Amendment of Sheriff Court Ordinary Cause, Summary Cause and Small Claim, Rules) 1990	S.I. 1990/661	Paragraph 4
Act of Sederunt (Amendment of Sheriff Court Ordinary Cause, Summary Cause and Small Claim, Rules) (No. 2) 1990	S.I. 1990/2105	Paragraph 4
Act of Sederunt (Amendment of Summary Cause and Small Claim Rules) 1991	S.I. 1991/821	Paragraph 3
Act of Sederunt (Amendment of Ordinary Cause, Summary Cause and Small Claim Rules) 1992	S.I. 1992/249	Paragraph 4
Act of Sederunt (Sheriff Court Ordinary Cause Rules) 1993	S.I. 1993/1956	Paragraph 4

SHERIFF COURTS (SCOTLAND) ACT 1971

Summary causes

[1]**35.**—(1) The definition of "summary cause" contained in paragraph (i) of section 3 of the Sheriff Courts (Scotland) Act 1907 shall cease to have effect, and for the purposes of the procedure and practice in civil proceedings in the sheriff court there shall be a form of process, to be known as a "summary cause", which shall be used for the purposes of all civil proceedings brought in that court, being proceedings of one or other of the following descriptions, namely—

[2](a)   actions for payment of money not exceeding one thousand five hundred pounds in amount (exclusive of interest and expenses);

[2](b)   actions of multiple poinding, actions of furthcoming and actions of sequestration for rent, where the value of the fund in medio, or the value of the arrested fund or subject, or the rent in respect of which sequestration is asked, as the case may be, does not exceed one thousand five hundred pounds (exclusive of interest and expenses);

[2,3](c)   actions ad factum praestandum and actions for the recovery of possession of heritable or moveable property, other than actions in which there is claimed in addition, or as an alternative, to a decree ad factum praestandum or for such recovery, as the case may be, a decree for payment of money exceeding one thousand five hundred pounds in amount (exclusive of interest and expenses);

(d)   proceedings which, according to the law and practice existing immediately before the commencement of this Act, might competently be brought in the sheriff's small debt court or were required to be conducted and disposed of in the summary manner in which proceedings were conducted and disposed of under the Small Debt Acts; and any reference in the following provisions of this Act, or in any other enactment (whether passed or made before or after the commencement of this Act) relating to civil procedure in the sheriff court, to a summary cause shall be construed as a reference to a summary cause within the meaning of this subsection.

[4](1A) For the avoidance of doubt it is hereby declared that nothing in subsection (1) above shall prevent the Court of Session from making

different rules of procedure and practice in relation to different descriptions of summary cause proceedings.

(2) There shall be a form of summary cause process, to be known as a "small claim", which shall be used for the purposes of such descriptions of summary cause proceedings as are prescribed by the Lord Advocate by order.

(3) No enactment or rule of law relating to admissibility or corroboration of evidence before a court of law shall be binding in a small claim.

(4) An order under subsection (2) above shall be by statutory instrument but shall not be made unless a draft of it has been approved by a resolution of each House of Parliament.

NOTE

1. As amended by Law Reform (Miscellaneous Provisions) (Scotland) Act 1985 (c.73), s.18(1).
2. As amended by S.I. 1988/1993, art.3.
3. Excluded by the Land Tenure Reform (Scotland) Act 1974 (c.38), s.9(6).
4. Inserted by the Law Reform (Miscellaneous Provisions) (Scotland) Act 1985 (c.73), s.59 and Sch.2, para.14.

Procedure in summary causes

36.—(1) In relation to summary causes the power conferred on the Court of Session by section 32 of this Act shall extend to the making of rules permitting a party to such a cause, in such circumstances as may be specified in the rule, to be represented by a person who is neither an advocate nor a solicitor.

(2) A summary cause shall be commenced by a summons in, or as nearly as is practicable in, such form as may be prescribed by rules under the said section 32.

[1](3) The evidence, if any, given in a summary cause shall not be recorded.

[2](4) [...]

NOTE

1. Excluded by Maintenance Orders (Reciprocal Enforcement) Act 1972 (c.18), s.4(4)(b).
2. Repealed by Debtors (Scotland) Act 1987 (c.18), s.108 and Sch.7, paras 5, 9(1), Sch.8.

Further provisions as to small claims

[1]**36A.** Where the pursuer in a small claim is not—

    (a) a partnership or a body corporate; or

(b) acting in a representative capacity,

he may require the sheriff clerk to effect service of the summons on his behalf.

NOTE
1. Inserted by Law Reform (Miscellaneous Provisions) (Scotland) Act 1985 (c.73), s.18(2).

Expenses in small claims

[1]**36B.**—(1) No award of expenses shall be made in a small claim in which the value of the claim does not exceed such sum as the Lord Advocate shall prescribe by order.

(2) Any expenses which the sheriff may award in any other small claim shall not exceed such sum as the Lord Advocate shall prescribe by order.

(3) Subsections (1) and (2) above do not apply to a party to a small claim—

(a) who being a defender—
  (i) has not stated a defence; or
  (ii) having stated a defence, has not proceeded with it; or
  (iii) having stated and proceeded with a defence, has not acted in good faith as to its merits; or
(b) on whose part there has been unreasonable conduct in relation to the proceedings or the claim; nor do they apply in relation to an appeal to the sheriff principal.

(4) An order under this section shall be by statutory instrument but shall not be made unless a draft of it has been approved by a resolution of each House of Parliament.

NOTE
1. Inserted by Law Reform (Miscellaneous Provisions) (Scotland) Act 1985 (c.73), s.18(2).

Remits

37.—(1) In the case of any ordinary cause brought in the sheriff court the sheriff—

(a) shall at any stage, on the joint motion of the parties to the cause, direct that the cause be treated as a summary cause, and in that case the cause shall be treated for all purposes (including appeal) as a summary cause and shall proceed accordingly;

(b) may, subject to section 7 of the Sheriff Courts (Scotland) Act 1907, on the motion of any of the parties to the cause, if he is of the opinion that the importance or difficulty of the cause make it appropriate to do so, remit the cause to the Court of Session.

(2) In the case of any summary cause, the sheriff at any stage—

(a) shall, on the joint motion of the parties to the cause, and
(b) may, on the motion of any of the parties to the cause, if he is of the opinion that the importance or difficulty of the cause makes it appropriate to do so,

direct that the cause be treated as an ordinary cause, and in that case the cause shall be treated for all purposes (including appeal) as an ordinary cause and shall proceed accordingly:

Provided that a direction under this subsection may, in the case of an action for the recovery of possession of heritable or moveable property, be given by the sheriff of his own accord.

[1](2A) In the case of any action in the sheriff court, being an action for divorce or an action in relation to parental responsibilities or parental rights (within the meaning of sections 1(3) and 2(4) respectively of the Children (Scotland) Act 1995) in relation to a child or the guardianship or adoption of a child the sheriff may, of his own accord, at any stage remit the action to the Court of Session.

(2B) In the case of any small claim the sheriff at any stage—

(a) may, if he is of the opinion that a difficult question of law or a question of fact of exceptional complexity is involved, of his own accord or on the motion of any party to the small claim;
(b) shall, on the joint motion of the parties to the small claim,

direct that the small claim be treated as a summary cause (not being a small claim) or ordinary cause, and in that case the small claim shall be treated for all purposes (including appeal) as a summary cause (not being a small claim) or ordinary cause as the case may be.

(2C) In the case of any cause which is not a small claim by reason only of any monetary limit applicable to a small claim or to summary causes, the sheriff at any stage shall, on the joint motion of the parties to the cause, direct that the cause be treated as a small claim and in that case the cause shall be treated for all purposes (including appeal) as a small claim and shall proceed accordingly.

(3) A decision—

(a) to remit, or not to remit, under subsection (2A) (2B) or (2C) above; or

(b) to make, or not to make, a direction by virtue of paragraph (b) of, or the proviso to, subsection (2) above, shall not be subject to review; but from a decision to remit, or not to remit, under subsection (1)(b) above an appeal shall lie to the Court of Session.

(4) In this section "sheriff" includes a sheriff principal.

NOTE
1. Amended by the Children (Scotland) Act 1995 (c.36), Sch.4, para.18(3).

Appeal in summary causes
[1]**38.** In the case of—

(a) any summary cause an appeal shall lie to the sheriff principal on any point of law from the final judgment of the sheriff; and

(b) any summary cause other than a small claim an appeal shall lie to the Court of Session on any point of law from the final judgment of the sheriff principal, if the sheriff principal certifies the cause as suitable for such an appeal, but save as aforesaid an interlocutor of the sheriff or the sheriff principal in any such cause shall not be subject to review.

NOTE
1. As amended by the Law Reform (Miscellaneous Provisions) (Scotland) Act 1985 (c.73), s.18(4). Excluded by Debtors (Scotland) Act 1987 (c.18), ss.103(1), 108(2) and Sch.7, paras 5, 9(1).

SMALL CLAIMS (SCOTLAND) ORDER 1988

(S.I. 1988/1999)

15th November 1988

The Lord Advocate, in exercise of the powers conferred on him by sections 35(2) and 36B(1) and (2) of the Sheriff Courts (Scotland) Act 1971, and of all other powers enabling him in that behalf, hereby makes the following Order, a draft of which has been laid before and approved by resolution of each House of Parliament:

Citation and commencement
1. This Order may be cited as the Small Claims (Scotland) Order 1988 and shall come into force on 30th November 1988.

Proceedings to be small claims
2. The form of summary cause process, to be known as a "small claim", shall be used for the purposes of summary cause proceedings of one or other of the following descriptions, namely—

(a) actions for payment of money not exceeding £750 in amount (exclusive of interest and expenses), other than actions in respect of aliment and interim aliment and actions of defamation;

(b) actions ad factum praestandum and actions for the recovery of possession of moveable property where in any such action ad factum praestandum or for recovery there is included, as an alternative to the claim, a claim for payment of a sum not exceeding £750 (exclusive of interest and expenses).

3. For the purpose of article 2, actions ad factum praestandum include actions for delivery and actions for implement but do not include actions for count, reckoning and payment.

Limit on award of expenses in small claims

4.—(1) The provisions of this article are without prejudice to the provisions of section 36B(3) of the Sheriff Courts (Scotland) Act 1971.

(2) No award of expenses shall be made in a small claim as specified in article 2 of this Order in which the value of the claim does not exceed £200.

(3) In the case of any small claim other than a small claim to which paragraph (2) applies, the sheriff may award expenses not exceeding £75.

INDEX